Praise for *Healing the Orphaned Heart...*

Every time we are wounded, the enemy whispers lies into our ears; and the lies become strongholds. "You are not worthy, you are not loved or lovable, no one wants you, no one likes you, you will never amount to anything, you are a loser." What we believe to be true, is true to us, even if it is a lie. Fear, shame, abandonment, and rejection enter into our mental attitude. As I point out in my book "My Father, My Son, Healing the Orphan Heart with the Father's love," only an experiential encounter with the Father's Love can displace Orphan Thinking.

My new book, "A Memoir: Healing Childhood Emotional Wounds, an Adult's Journey to God's Love," follows the journey of an emotionally wounded American boy through his childhood to wounded adulthood and his ultimate inner healing. As I point out, there must be a transformation of mind knowledge into heart knowledge.

Janet encountered a unique set of cultural circumstances that required special methodologies of healing the orphaned heart in Africa. God's divine inspiration led her on a journey to successfully minister to children where she has taken healing the Orphaned Heart to new levels of understanding. Journey through the pages and let that understanding change your life and then help others.

- Bruce Brodowski, author of *A Memoir: Healing Childhood Emotional Wounds, an Adult's Journey to God's Love*

I read my friend, Janet Helms' exciting, life-changing work, *Healing the Orphaned Heart,* as quickly as I could. I hope you too will read about her life's challenges and how specific prayers and Scriptures given to her brought her through each one to victory. Her great ongoing mission's ministry is to orphans in Uganda and Kenya. You can be a part of it too, like Janet and her husband, Worth, who are spiritual parents. Find the details in this inspiring, Spirit-filled book, *Healing The Orphaned Heart.*

   - Dr. Rita Bennett, D.Litt. author of *You Can be Emotionally Free*

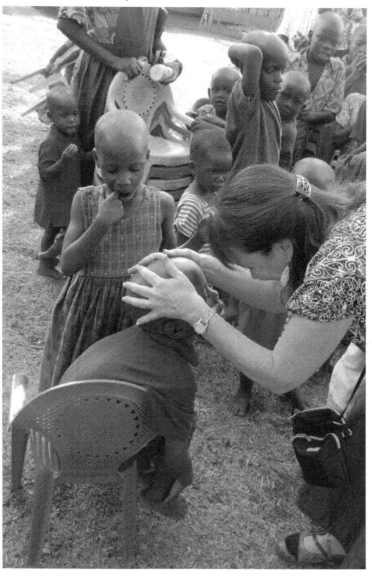

Healing the Orphaned Heart
by Janet Helms
Copyright ©2016 Janet Helms

ISBN 978-1-63360-033-1
For Worldwide Distribution

Printed in the U.S.A.

I dedicate this book to the memory of my pastor and mentor, Reverend Mike Henning, who gave me the prayers that changed me from the inside out, starting with, "Lord, make me the woman You want me to be." Thank you, Mike, for your faithful counsel and guidance.

Table of Contents

Foreword

This book is my story of how I uncovered a powerful truth that has already helped many people the world over. My ministry objective in writing this book is that many people will be aware of, and then healed from, what I have come to call an Orphaned Heart. It's already an epidemic around the world and is usually caused by traumatic life events such as divorce, absentee fathers, and child abuse. Many children who are acting out their pain are often from broken homes or orphaned situations. There may be adults present in their lives, but they are lonely and feel as if it is their lot for the remainder of their days. They are afraid, angry and searching for love, often in all the wrong places.

In Africa, as well as the United States, I have found people who have wholeheartedly embraced the reality of this concept, having seen and felt its cause and effect. A pastor from the Congo exclaimed to all at my first Orphaned Heart conference in 2011: "We have known we are suffering from something here in Africa, but we never knew the name of it. Now we know — it's the Orphaned Heart." He went on to say, "We suffer from it and you can see its effects everywhere, from genocide, to war, to orphans, and even in polygamy. We can see it in every aspect of life and culture, and now we know what it is."

When we held that first conference, the Holy Spirit had led me to something powerful. I felt as if people were coming to a banquet. They were hungry and searching for something to nourish and help them grow. The conference was the banquet hall and they feasted on everything that was taught. There has been much healing every time I have been there to conduct a conference. What's more, I see the healing results in the U.S. as well as in Africa. My teaching, seminars, plays, and counseling have helped shape the content and direction of this book, which contains my life story and how I came to know and teach about the Orphaned Heart.

In these pages, I will share with you how I came upon this insight. I will also share my testimony of how God called me to minister, and introduce you to the people who contributed to my development and understanding. God was involved in every part of it, and I want to share that so you know not only the message but also His messenger.

Jesus is referred to as Emmanuel, which means God With Us. He is the Word made flesh who dwelled among us. We have a God who is not just Spirit; we have a God who has the same flesh as we do! A teaching like the Orphaned Heart is something that is a practical word that emanates from God's heart, and it has taken on a real and tangible form in my life and the lives of others who teach and have been impacted by its message.

I've sold insurance my entire adult life, but that is not who I am. My insurance sales provide for my ministry in many ways. I'm grateful for my work, but this book is what I am all about, and will serve as an important part of my legacy. I want this message to go out far and wide and live longer than I do. I don't see the Orphaned Heart problem becoming any less of a problem, but only magnifying in the coming years.

I am now so aware of this problem that it seems at times that I have a spiritual radar to help identify those with an Orphaned Heart. I can see it in their eyes and in their countenance. I hear it in what they say. I want to help you have the same kind of sensitivity and capability to identify and apply the remedy for the Orphaned Heart. Whatever God does with this project is up to Him. I hope to have a manual soon to fulfill the requests of many from Africa. I need to begin with this book, however, and start the process that will allow the message to spread far and wide.

First, I would like to thank my editor, John Stanko, because he provided the spark for this project. I have known John for many years, and we have talked about a book during that time. John challenged me that this was the time to do it. I appreciate everything he has done for me to help me find and embrace my purpose – giving my life deep meaning.

Then I want to thank my spiritually adopted Ugandan daughter, Olive Nyamuhunge, because without her I would not be as familiar with the pain of the Orphaned Heart as I am. Through her life, I saw the changes that can occur when an orphan has someone to trust and depend on to be there for her. It's difficult for an orphan to trust because they have been let down too many times. I've been involved with Olive on a close, personal level, and have watched her transformation through her connection to two loving families — one in the States and the other in Uganda.

Then there is Sylvia Tamusuza. She was important and instrumental in my development as we worked together to educate orphans in Uganda. Sylvia brought to my attention many of the issues orphans face because she saw them in the Love and Care Family organization she started. Sylvia taught me that you can educate orphans, but they will never change until they are set free from the spirit of rejection and abandonment, from the wounds of the Orphaned Heart. Sylvia was Olive's foster mother from ages nine to twenty, and we raised Olive together across the ocean.

Of course, there's my precious husband, Worth Helms. He got me started doing my musical shows and served as my agent, which we will talk about at length later in this book. I am so glad I agreed to go on that blind date! Through our relationship, God has truly molded me into the woman He wanted me to be.

Thanks also go out to Lillian Novak, the woman who confirmed and guided my intimate relationship with the Lord at age five. I must also acknowledge Mike Henning, rector at Saint Stephen's Church, who passed away in September of 1994. You will read about the role he played in my becoming the woman God wanted me to be.

Reverend Qampicha Daniel Wario is a Kenyan pastor, now the bishop of the Anglican diocese of Marsabit, who I met in seminary, and our relationship has become a close partnership as we work toward building a school in northern Kenya. He is a son of my heart. When I was called to start the school with Qampicha, I distinctly heard the word "benefactor" in my heart. I knew I was to be a benefactor for the project, but it has turned out to become so much more for me.

Another person who impacted me along the way was Dr. Sam Annankra from Ghana. He passed away in 2007 from hepatitis, and I will share more about him later. I learned from Sam the spiritual disciplines necessary to grow in faith. Sam ended up living with us on and off for a year and a half when he was being treated for cancer, and I watched him face his disease in our home. Many people would visit our home to be prayed over by him. I witnessed firsthand the amount of time he spent reading the Bible and in prayer every morning. He was also an anointed evangelist who would speak of Jesus to individuals everywhere we went. Sam taught me the attributes necessary to accept and fulfill my calling to ministry.

Reid Carpenter believed in the Holy Spirit power of this message before there was much to show for it — just the idea and the Hope Fellowship which was just started. He believed in me and the message, and has supported it in many important ways. I thank him for his steadfast help and inspired and vital mentorship.

Rev. John Guest was my evangelistic pastor as a teenager in high school. I marvel how he has been there at critical junctures of my life: from taking Americans on a trip to the Holy Land where God spoke to me very concretely; to the bedside of my father when he died; and, preaching at the "going away party" that my mother hosted as she faced death from cancer. He performed Worth's and my marriage ceremony and also had the passion to take a group of Americans to Uganda in 1999 — where we met Olive. From there, our lives became deeply embedded in East Africa where my ministry has been planted and has grown in its rich soil of faith. Thank you, John, for listening to God and going where He called you – bringing many of us along.

Bishop John Guernsey, who loves Africa and is committed there, yet loves his flock here in the States, has been an inspiration to me. He has mentored me from the beginning of this message and not only me, but also even met with my team in East Africa. He makes himself available and has focused me to strategically think how to spread this message.

I have admired Rita Bennett since I first went to one of her conferences in Seattle in 2008. She has been a real leader in the concept of inner-healing prayer. Her gift to put these unusual subjects involving the Holy Spirit in easy-to-read formats has made inner-healing prayer accessible. I also appreciate the training and insight of Judith MacNutt and Valerie Vitunic.

While at Trinity School for Ministry, God used two professors: The first is Reverend Dr. John Macdonald, my advisor who taught Missions and took groups of students to Sololo, Kenya, where KCEP partnered to build Tumaini Academy. I also want to acknowledge His Grace, Rev. Dr. Grant LeMarquand, who is now the Bishop of the Horn of Africa, who was my professor in 2012. He agreed to help me in my final three-credit independent study on *Healing the Orphaned Heart in East Africa*. It began to focus me on this healing message. A big thank you also goes to Rev. Christopher Klukas, the head of Communications, who has advised me about social media and designed the Orphaned Heart website.

I am an American, and can only visit Africa from time to time. Therefore, I have needed a solid, committed team in Africa who were willing and capable of establishing the work there. I would like to thank Rev. Simon Peter Dembe who helped found the Orphaned Heart Ministry in East Africa. He is a beloved spiritual son of mine. You will read his testimony later, but I am grateful that someone who has been deeply helped by the message is able to spread the word and help others. My thanks also goes to Reverend Susan Olwa, the patron of the HOPE Fellowship on the campus of Uganda Christian University (UCU). She has a deep compassion, call, and commitment to help the students, and her wisdom is something I rely on frequently. I respect and love her. I must acknowledge the important role Joseph Musaalo, the lead counselor at UCU played in this journey. He immediately responded to the message and agreed to be our first Patron at UCU. He called me the "vision bearer," and I embraced the words and the role once he spoke them. And of course, there are Paul Agaba, Charlotte Fiona Namanya, Ronnie Mutegeki, Winnefred Abudo, and Emmanuel Mujuni, the core team of the Healing Delegation, who have worked so well together.

In Rwanda, I thank Archbishop Onesphore Rwaje for his leadership in supporting us in this mission; Rev. Francis Karemera, the Provincial Secretary of Rwanda, who has a vision for this ministry and never wavered in his belief of what God could do; the Venerable Reverend Louis Pasteur Kabayiza for being the first to come along side me in this vision; Eric Mwizerwa, who honored me by asking me to be his mother in his wedding and also to be at the baptism of his daughter. We believe Rwanda will be a strategic and important focus for this healing message because we have such support and agreement from those in top leadership. Praise God!

I would especially like to thank the Anglican Diocese of Pittsburgh who added Orphaned Heart Ministries as one of their missions, making it possible for donors to make tax deductible contributions through them and while giving our mission their "stamp of approval".

I thank God for my father and mother, John and Bea Mouganis, who had strong faith and went to church with us all through our lives, giving us a family culture and a foundation of active Christian faith. Their legacy of faith is a rock in the lives of my sister, Nancy, and brother, John, who are also strong believers, as are their children. I also thank God for my wonderful network of loving, Christian friends and intercessors who have been there for me at each bend in the road. That is the power of a community of believers around us in our pilgrim's walk on this earth.

There you have a bit of who I am and to whom I am indebted. Yet I have only scratched the surface. There is much more in the pages to come that will introduce you to my message, my friends and mentors, and my journey. I pray that this book will contribute to your own healing if the need is there, and will also equip you to recognize and speak healing to the Orphaned Heart in your world. And now, let me tell you my story of how God equipped and released me to confront and heal the Orphaned Heart.

Janet Helms
Pittsburgh, PA
April 2016

Introduction

I developed a show earlier in my ministry that was called *Lord, Make Me the Woman You Want Me to Be*. In 2006, I found myself performing this show at Uganda Christian University with the help of my friend Sylvia Tamusuza, whom I met while she was in graduate school in my hometown of Pittsburgh, PA. We were expecting 1,500 people for the show, and we were not disappointed. We thought everything was "set," although in an African context, nothing is ever really set. Things were in their usual state of flux as we prepared to go on stage.

We had a wonderful keyboardist and a group of technical workers from the university who were all capable people. Sylvia and I had rehearsed with them the day before to set all our tech cues, and each one had a marked script to follow. We thought everything would be fine, especially after we bathed the event in one final gathering for prayer. I forgot that when you pray for something, it doesn't mean it all works out perfectly!

I went on stage after an introduction and things fell apart during my opening monologue when I was talking to God. In my talk, I called Him "Lord." People told me later that they didn't understand the word "Lord." They thought I was saying "Lloyd." Right away there was a disconnect and the students started laughing, not knowing to whom I was talking.

The show began with a solo, but the students were making so much noise that I could not hear my cues. Thus, I was out of sync with the musicians. People started giggling and it spread through the audience. What's more, I have a voice that is classically trained, and that's not something they hear very often. To my embarrassment, they started mimicking me.

The audience noise increased to the point that the techies and musicians couldn't hear me, I couldn't hear the music, and it seemed like everyone was laughing and talking. We could not get in sync, and the laughing and heckling got louder and louder. I felt totally naked in front of them and, for the first time in my life, I felt true and total humiliation.

I didn't know how to get off the stage, but I didn't want to just walk off. Sylvia was waiting for her cue to enter the stage. I kept gesturing to her to get on the stage and help me, but she didn't want to come out. Then I would go back out and do my best to be heard, but to no avail. It was about as much of a disaster as a show could be. I felt as if verbal tomatoes – if there is such a thing – were being hurled at me.

Ironically, I kept thinking about the verse in which Paul talked about being a fool for Christ (see 1 Corinthians 4:10), and that is what kept me on stage. I certainly felt like a total fool and so empty — there was nothing of me, nothing of Janet left. I had felt humbled before in life, but this humiliation was different, and it seemed that it would never end.

Finally, Sylvia came on stage and, because they were more accustomed to her accent, things improved. As I look back on that event, which I have done many times since that day, I see that God had begun to prepare me for what was going to happen. When Sylvia and I were rehearsing, she was telling me about a difficult challenge with one of the orphans whom she was trying to help. She said that we could try to educate these orphaned children all day long, but they would never change because they suffered from a spirit of rejection and abandonment. That point struck deep within me.

In my mind, I wondered how we could include that statement or address that issue in the show. Little did I know God would show me how to do that during that university performance, and confirm during that 2006 trip how true Sylvia's insight was. As I paid attention to the audience, I began to see it in the eyes of those young people who were laughing. I didn't know how to address or heal it, but I saw it — the loneliness, the abandonment, and the pain.

At one point I actually said, "I've never been treated so rudely in my life. I'm just going to stop performing right now. I can't take it." There was so much confusion that I don't even think anyone heard me. We found a way to end it, which I don't even remember, because the show was so far gone. At the end of the show, we ran off the stage. People applauded but I was too weary to care; I just wanted to get off stage. In my mind, all 1,500 had been laughing at me. In retrospect, there were actually people watching and listening, in spite of all the problems. After it was over, Sylvia did as we planned, and took a microphone to ask anyone who wanted to talk about the orphan problem in Uganda to stay behind.

She started a dialogue with the people who stayed (and there were about 300) while I went off to the side of the auditorium and cried. As I reflect on it, (and I don't know any other way to say this), I now see that God literally slapped me into the reality of why we were there in the first place. It wasn't for the performance; it was to talk about the orphan situation. It was only then I noticed that Sylvia was doing a good job of getting people to talk and give some testimonies about their experiences as orphans. That in and of itself was a major breakthrough, because Africans generally don't share about the orphan issue.

Being an orphan is a source of shame for them because the word for orphan is similar to the word in their culture used to describe discarding garbage. No one wants to admit that they were treated like trash, so they stay silent. In that auditorium, I heard students, who were just a few minutes ago laughing me off stage, openly sharing their testimonies, and I was moved. As the session was coming to a close, I went to the microphone and asked how many would be interested in starting a support group where students could share their problems. I used the American word "support," but later learned that it wasn't the best word to use. Eventually, we referred to it as a fellowship group.

Other good things happened that night as well as after the show's failure. I suggested we have a concert of prayer about the orphan problems. We broke into groups of seven or eight and prayed beautiful prayers. As we were praying for the orphans, I felt it was like incense going up to the nostrils of God. We truly had a concert of prayer. Then when we asked how many would like to sign up for the fellowship group, to our amazement, about 100 students signed up to be part of a group. That was the beginning of what today we call the Hope Fellowship. My concert turned in a few minutes from an abysmal failure to a colossal success!

As we were leaving, one more amazing thing took place. A lovely young girl came up to me and sweetly said, "Your tears broke us." I realized that some strange spiritual transaction had happened during the event. As I described earlier, there was nothing left of me after that event. But God chose me as His vessel and resurrected my shame and embarrassment into the beginning of an incredible healing journey for many people. He could do that because I was void of everything, even my identity. God used it all for His purpose, and still uses that musical performance to this day.

In 2011, I led my first conference in Africa that featured focused teaching on the Orphaned Heart. One of my friends who was with me on that trip was reflecting on what I told her about that performance in 2006. My friend believed that people were set free in 2006 because they were able to put their rejection and abandonment on me. That was a big spiritual lesson for me concerning what it's like to model Christ for others.

I gained another insight from the failed performance, and that was what it was like to be a Christian, which literally means to be a "little Christ." Of all the roles

I ever played or thought of playing in a theater or in life, I never thought that playing the fool for Christ would be the beginning of an amazing ministry. Christ was humiliated on the Cross, but that's where our redemption comes from. My painful failure was nothing compared to Christ's sacrifice, but God used it, and I marvel at what He did! That day was the genesis of my ministry that brings healing to orphans.

If I were to choose a verse from the Bible that summarized my work with orphans, it would be John 14:18, when Jesus said, "I will no longer leave you as orphans. I will come to you." The work Jesus did on the Cross enabled us to become children of God and enjoy an intimate relationship with God the Father through the Holy Spirit. After I was emptied, I could hear God better than I ever had. I am glad to report that the orphan fellowship is still going on, and the acronym HOPE in the Hope Fellowship stands for "Healing, Overcoming, Prayer and Empowerment."

The fellowship groups that were started that day became a wonderful source of help and spiritual growth for the students. Even in its infancy, the Fellowship gave the students a safe place where healing could take place in their hearts. Some of the students told me that when they learned how to be healed after coming together, they could then go back and share it with their home villages. That's what is so great about a college setting. When young people are touched, they have energy to reproduce what they have learned. People went back to their towns and villages to share how to heal from the Orphaned Heart, and that was the beginning of my work in East Africa.

Yet my ministry didn't start in 2006. That is when

it made its debut. Now I realize that God was preparing me for this work long before 2006. If you will permit me, I would like to go back and share with you my journey prior to 2006 in Section One. Then I would like to tell you about what happened after 2006 up to the writing of this book in Section Two. In Section Three, I will share in more detail what I have learned and what I (and you) can teach about the Orphaned Heart.

My hope as you read is that you will be equipped to identify any Orphaned Heart symptoms in your own life and in the lives of others. I also hope that my journey will encourage you in your journey as you seek to find a message of hope and healing for others. Your message doesn't have to be like mine, it just has to be real with the power to help others as you tell your story. In other words, I want to tell my story to free you to tell yours. Let's go back then, all the way to the early years of my life, and learn how I came to understand this painful truth of the Orphaned Heart, and the wonderful plan that God set forth in Christ to heal it.

SECTION ONE

•

THE PREPARATION YEARS

Chapter 1

Lillian

In some ways, I am an unlikely candidate to write about something like the Orphaned Heart because I had a wonderful childhood. I could feel God's presence when I was outdoors and I didn't really have to identify who or what it was. It was just the joy of the Lord as I was outside running, skipping and leaping. It was freedom, a freedom that I knew God wanted me to have. A woman named Lillian Novak played an important role early in my life. When I was six years old, Lillian was in a prayer group with my mom. Lillian had an amazing attic that was filled with wonders for children, and she had a fertile, active imagination.

Children need to have their imagination stimulated in order to understand God, which is why, by the way, children have a fascination with C.S. Lewis' fictional stories. I was blessed that someone like Lillian came along who was able to fan the flame of my creative imagination into a full-fledged fire! I fell in love with God when I was a child, and that's the thing that kept me going and growing. I can still feel that same sense of God's presence today, the feeling like I'm running and jumping in God's presence.

It also seems odd that God would call me to this ministry because my mother and father had a wonderful marriage. They weren't perfect, but they were great parents who loved each other and provided a stable home in every way. I have a precious sister Nancy, and she also has a vivid imagination, just like me. She is older than I am and has been quite a support to me in all of my ministries.

My brother is ten years younger than I and someone who was quite different than my sister and me. We didn't quite understand him because he was always playing with trucks and was interested in so many different things. Today, I am glad I had a brother to watch and learn from. We all grew up in Western Pennsylvania, which is still home for me. My siblings are believers, as are their families.

I started playing the piano at the age of six when my mother gave me lessons. It was a pretty dismal experience for me. My mother hired Miss Turbush as my piano teacher. She would come to the house once a week, but I never practiced. I will never forget Miss Turbush's shoes, which had thick heels with a bow that seemed so odd to me. I took lessons for so long that my love for music eventually developed. Then I started singing in musicals and being part of dramatic presentations. My mother had done a lot of theater in college, so it was a natural thing for me to do that as well. I loved performing, and I was cast in the lead role in many musicals. And today, I wish I had taken my piano lessons with Miss Turbush more seriously!

When I would go to Lilian's home, she let me see what she called her prayer attic. She had many wonderful pictures of Jesus and symbols of the faith there, and she would tell me about an elf who lived there in her attic. At the age of five, I was really intrigued by the elf. I wanted to go up to the attic to see if I could catch him. I still have letters that Lillian wrote me about the elf and what he was doing on the day she wrote them. She would put silly things in those letters, things like the elf said hello to me, or that she had just had lunch or tea with him.

I was delighted to have an adult talk to me about an elf, which made me even more intrigued with her prayer attic. Lillian got down to my level and used her imagination, which in turn sparked mine. Then one day in Sunday School, I was coloring a picture of Jesus. The teacher told us that Jesus loves us, and that He wanted us to be good. She told us we should do what Jesus wanted us to do and be nice boys and girls.

My feeling was that she was describing someone who was watered down and not at all the kind of relationship I had with the Lord. It may sound strange, but I had a crisis of faith at that early age because I wondered if maybe God was only part of my imagination and did not really exist. No adult was describing this love relationship I had with Him, so I feared maybe my imagination was making it all up.

One day my mom took me to her Bible study and I asked Lillian about God. She was sitting on her pink couch, the room covered with pink shag carpet, which was all so like Lillian. I asked her what God was like and she extended her arms and said, "God is like the sun. His light lights your life and His warmth enfolds you."

That description impacted me deeply, for it described the exact feeling I had when I felt God's presence as I was playing outdoors and sensed Him close to me. It felt as if He was running, jumping and skipping with me. God was my play partner, and it surprised me that Lillian validated what I had been feeling. I did not find that validation in Sunday School, only in Lillian's Bible study. When Lillian said that, I knew that God existed and I never questioned that again.

Lillian and I remained close over the years, and she served as my childhood mentor. By the time I was 16, I had outgrown the thought of there being an elf in her attic, but I never outgrew my ability to use my imagination when she was around. Lillian had me come to her house to find all kinds of treasures, using a map she had created for my use. She called it her prayer treasure map and it led to spiritual treasures. When I found one thing, there was a clue leading to the next somewhere in her house. That was what Lillian did, depict things full of God, using creativity and imagination that required play and produced fun.

My sister Nancy also participated in all of that and we both loved Lillian. Lillian would hear from God and sometimes she'd ask us to go to places where she was called to pray, which often was a church. I was a teenager and we would go inside and pray with her as she felt led to pray. She called those trips and prayer journeys "Lion Tasks." Those are my most vivid memories of my teenage years, going with her and doing those Lion Tasks, where we would often pray for the world — or for that church. I was so in love with the character Aslan, the lion hero in the C.S. Lewis books. I identified most closely with Lucy in those books because she had a deep, intimate relationship with Aslan the lion. The Lion Tasks fell right in line with the image of Lucy and Aslan that I imagined.

After high school, I attended Grove City College, a Christian school close to home in Western Pennsylvania. I stayed in touch with Lillian as much as I could. As I matured, Lillian's role in my life changed, and she then imparted a depth of theology to me that was real and lasting. We studied the Bible when we were together, and did other spiritual things as a team. Even Lillian's death had a profound impact on me.

I never knew Lillian to be sick until her death in 1984 when she died on a pilgrimage to the Holy Land. She went on a tour with her daughter, an Episcopal priest, to Israel along with other Episcopal priests, including my pastor, John Guest, his wife Kathie, and a few bishops. Lillian went to accompany her daughter, but ended up dying by the Sea of Galilee. As my pastor, John went on to have a profound impact on my life. I will share more about him later.

Lillian's death was quite a shock to everyone, and I don't think her daughte3r knew exactly what to do. She decided to bury her in the Holy Land, and people who witnessed the burial said it was a remarkable time of prayer and worship. John and Kathie Guest say that to this day the burial was one of the most spiritual moments of their lives as they buried her at night in the Holy Land. Of course, I was saddened and shocked at her passing and I thought I would only have Lillian's memories to guide and comfort me as I grew older. Little did I know that I would make my own trip to the Holy Land years later and that Lillian would once again impact me there as she had here in the States.

Chapter 2

My Trip to
the Holy Land

In 1993, my parents decided to take my niece, my brother, and me on a trip to Israel led by Rector John Guest, who would lead devotions. There were a lot of people on that trip, but the time leading up to my pilgrimage to the Holy Land was one of the saddest times of my life.

I had turned 40 years of age the December before we left, and I had been divorced for eight years at that point. I was stuck in life, doing the same old job and not making any progress on any front. My friend and rector at St. Stephen's church, Mike Henning, knew I was struggling and recommended a prayer that he had known women to pray with great results. The prayer was simple: "Lord, make me the woman You want me to be." I started praying that prayer and got immediate results, although not what I expected at all. I had been dating a man for six years who broke up with me after I started praying that prayer.

It was December, and as a soloist in the church, I was part of the Christmas Eve service. During the service, while seated up front, I was silently crying. Most people in the audience had no idea what was going on, thinking maybe I was overcome with the emotion of the Christmas season. Mike, however, knew that something was wrong and met with me after the service to find out what it was. I told him about my romantic breakup, and how difficult it was to face my age with no prospects of marriage. Mike then asked me if I could picture myself being the woman God wanted me to be if I was with that man. I thought for a moment, and then honestly had to say, "No," but it was still painful for me to face the loneliness. Mike then gave me a second prayer that he wanted me to use, and it was also simple: "Thank You, Lord, for the pain," because I was hurting.

Mike told me to thank God for the pain, and thank Him that this man had broken off our relationship, explaining that I had desired to do the will of God and God was helping me, even if I could not see that. In some ways, I had built my life on sand instead of rock, and since my divorce, I had not been living in the fullness of the Christian life. When I prayed the prayer for God to make me the woman He wanted me to be, my fake world came tumbling down.

All the lies I had believed and built my life on were revealed for what they were – unreality. You may be asking what kind of lies I was believing? They were not doctrinal lies, but rather falsehoods of how God worked and what He wanted from me. I was assuming that if God would change the things around me, then I would be able to change. If he gave me a husband, then I could serve Him more effectively. If He gave me a better job, then I could become more of who He wanted me to be. In that season of my life, I learned the difficult truth that God wants to change you and me on the inside, and then and only then do we qualify for things changing on the outside.

It wasn't only the relationship ending, for there were other changes that were occurring around me all at once. God was cleansing me of wrong thinking and attitudes, and His refiner's fire was producing tremendous change in my life. That prayer was as effective as Mike had promised, and this was happening right before my trip in February to Israel.

I confess that there was another reason I started praying that prayer: I wanted to have children. I had just turned 40, and I had told Mike back in December before the trip that I was angry with God because I felt God had given me this desire for children and I could not have any. I asked Mike why God had given me this desire in the first place. I wasn't likely to have any at that point, since I was 40 and the man I had dated for six years had gone away.

Mike explained that it's a godly desire to want children — God had indeed given it to me. He went on to explain that anything from God can be sacrificed and given back to Him for His purpose and glory. Mike gave me another prayer to go along with the make-me-the-woman prayer, and it went like this: "Thank You, Lord, for the desire to have children. I offer it back as a sacrifice that You can fulfill in any way You so desire." My prayer journal was filling up with simple prayers that Mike gave me!

I started praying that prayer and I sensed an immediate change in my feeling toward God. I was angry, but when I started employing that prayer, it didn't take long for it to change the dynamic between God and me. Immediately I felt my anger lift, and I began to trust God again. I put my desire for marriage and children in His hands, to accomplish when and how He saw fit. With my anger toward God gone, my life was better because I had peace. Life became much easier from that time forward. Then it was time for the pilgrimage to Israel.

At many sites in the Holy Land, Pastor Guest gave a short sermon on the biblical significance of the venue. That is why you never read the Bible the same way again after you have been to Israel, because you can see all the places where Jesus talked and walked. At one site, I had another unusual prayer encounter when God took the reins of my life back – it changed the course of my life.

I connected with a friend on the trip named Dotty, who was divorced like me. Our group was visiting the Church of the Sephulchre on the site where Catholics believe Jesus' crucifixion took place. John Guest asked Dotty and me to come forward because he said he wanted to pray that we would find our husbands in 1994. There we were, standing where Jesus had probably died on the Cross, and John prayed for us to have godly husbands. The good news is that John's prayer was fulfilled for both of us in the exact year of his request – 1994. I met my husband the following October, and Dotty married a man she already casually knew. I am happy to report that we both have great marriages to this day.

I reported in Chapter One that my childhood mentor, Lillian, was buried in Israel ten years before I arrived. I had not thought about visiting her gravesite, but when we were at the Sea of Galilee, Kathie Guest asked me, my mother and my 13-year-old niece, Stephanie, if we would like to see it. "Of course," we exclaimed, "we would love to visit it." It wasn't the reason I had come, but it ended up being an important part of my pilgrimage.

We found a taxi and were driving around, not really certain of exactly where to go. We eventually came to a place where there was a small hill on our left and the Sea of Galilee on our right. There was a knoll between us and the Sea and, to my surprise, Kathie said she thought the grave was at that specific spot. We couldn't see any markers, but we got out and climbed up the knoll. There at the top were five slabs of cement that could not be seen from the road. Sure enough, one said, "Here lies Lillian Novak by the Sea of Galilee." It included a passage from Mark where Jesus called His disciples by the Sea of Galilee: "He called them, and they left their father Zebedee in the boat with the hired men and followed him" (Mark 1:20).

As I was standing there, I had a sense that God was passing me a baton, that I was going to be involved in outreach, teaching, and evangelism, similar to what Lillian had done. He was asking me to be a vessel of healing and hope to touch the hearts of others. I didn't fully understand all that it meant, but I knew something spiritual was taking place. I was called to ministry by the Sea of Galilee, just like the disciples had been.

Lillian wasn't someone to get up and do an altar call as John Guest would do. She made herself available to the Holy Spirit so that when she spoke, it was exactly what the other person needed to hear. I saw her do that with people again and again. God was passing that gift on to me. I was not going to preach and call people to Christ, but I would provide a word in season that would help clear the way for God to use the people to whom I spoke.

Needless to say, that day was an important direction sign on my path of life. I had not intended for it to happen, but God used Kathie to get me to a place where He could speak to me.

While we were in Israel, I was asked to sing at some of the places we visited. One such place was a venue in Jerusalem where the Lord's Prayer is commemorated. It's an outdoor courtyard with tablets on the walls that contain the Lord's prayer in different languages. While I was there, a beggar was at the site. He went around to everyone and seemed to focus especially on me, grabbing and pulling at my sleeve. I asked the Lord to get this man out of there because he was ruining my holy moment, and using this holy site for his own monetary gain.

They asked me to sing the Lord's Prayer and I sang it acappella. I was standing under a tree with the sun shining into my eyes as I was singing it. After I was done, the team started walking toward the building, but once again I felt the beggar pulling on my shirt. I looked down at this short little man, and saw tears streaming down his face. He put his hand on his heart and bowed repeatedly while backing away from me. I can still see that scene in my mind's eye as I write.

I was so moved by what I had seen and heard that I ran to John and asked if he had seen what had happened. John told me it was a true miracle because that beggar was deaf and dumb, and God had opened his ears to hear me sing! That encounter proved to me that God had indeed given me a gift to reach others just as Lillian had. She didn't sing but she was creative in other ways, and that day my creativity touched that beggar. I knew it had nothing to do with my voice or how I sang the song. God had used

14

my singing to touch the heart of a beggar who had been there for who knows how many years, trying to get money from people. Maybe he had never been touched by the Lord as he had been in that moment.

I also learned on that Israel trip the truth of what my friend John Stanko says about travel and missions, "When you gotta go, you gotta go!" God spoke to me in Israel in a way that He could not have done in America. If I had not gone, I would have missed what God had for me. There are some who say, "If God wants to speak to me, I am right here." They don't go because they are afraid, or don't want to spend the time and money, or any other excuse they may concoct. God knows what He wants to say, but always chooses the setting where you and I can hear it best.

That is why I have to go to Africa as often as I do. Not only do I have to minister to the people there as Lillian would have done, but I also have to go and hear the voice of God for myself. I had to go hear and understand my calling. Don't tell God where and how He has to reveal Himself to you. You go where He directs, and listen when you go. That has been how I have done it since Israel, and I don't see that changing any time soon.

I heard a sermon once about how Saul, later to become the Apostle Paul, had to leave where he was to travel to Damascus, only to see the risen Christ on his way. There is something about having to be away from your normal surroundings in order to be more attentive to what God wants. When Jesus rose from the dead, he met with the disciples. They were all in Jerusalem, but He said He would meet them in Galilee.

Today, that's a two-hour bus trip from Jerusalem,

but back then it would have been an all-day journey. You may ask why He didn't talk to the disciples right then and there in Jerusalem. There is something about being in motion, moving and responding to God, that releases a dynamic of the Holy Spirit that is important. We are His vessels and His tabernacle. Where we go, God goes with us, but when we go, we are more attentive to His presence to which we may have grown accustomed.

The Incarnation is the word made flesh. Jesus didn't just send the word, He brought the word. He didn't send a book or a movie, God sent His Son! And when we go, He goes with us to reveal Himself to us. That's what happened to me in Israel, and it's been happening ever since, just like it did at Uganda Christian University in Kampala. There are plenty more prayers, signposts, and trips on which God spoke to me, but for now, let me tell you about what happened back home after that amazing time in Israel.

Chapter 3

My Worth

When I came back from the Holy Land, I discovered that Pastor Mike Henning's cancer of the esophagus had come back. He was very sick and the entire church was praying for him, but shortly thereafter he passed away tragically at the young age of 45. He had played such an important role in my life through his advice and the prayers that had so quickly impacted my life. At his funeral, I remember wondering who was going to have the same role he had played in my life. I was going to miss Mike, along with his friendship and counsel.

It was a beautiful funeral for an amazing man, and when I came home, I went crying into my bedroom, asking the Lord who was going to give me the next prayer. Then I realized that was selfish, and knew that God could give me words to pray without anyone's help. I realized that I could take the prayer Mike had given me about having children and insert the word "married" to say, "Thank you, Lord, for the desire to be married. I offer it back as a sacrifice to you. Fulfill it in any way you so desire." I reasoned that if God wanted me to have children, He obviously wanted me to be married. Of course, I reminded God that I was 40 and the biological clock was ticking.

I got down on my knees to utter that edited prayer, but I stopped mid-prayer and couldn't say the word "married" because I knew it was a lie. I couldn't lie to God and I couldn't lie to myself. I recognized then and there that I really didn't want to get married. The thought that I did not want to marry struck me like a huge lightning bolt. I was afraid my marriage wouldn't work out since the first one had ended in divorce. That had been a painful experience for me as a Christian, and I didn't want to go through that again. I was further confronted with the thought of my being unworthy of whoever God might want me to have.

I realized it had been a common pattern in my life to date people who were not good candidates to be my life partner. I was setting myself up for failure because I was afraid, pure and simple. I also knew I did not feel worthy of the kind of man God would want for me. I decided to pray a more basic prayer that the Lord would help me overcome my fear and give me the desire to be married. That's what I prayed in my bedroom after Mike's funeral: "God, give me the desire and willingness to be married to whomever you have for me!"

One month later, some friends told me they wanted to introduce me to a man they thought I would be interested in, so I agreed to a blind date. My date called me on the phone and, when he told me his name, Worth Helms, I had to ask him to say it again. Worth invited me to accompany him to a fundraiser, which had an entrance fee of $150 per person because the prizes being given away were supposed to be mink coats!

Then he asked me if he really needed to wear a suit and tie, and I told him I didn't really care what he wore, but I thought it may be a dressy event. He said he rarely wore suits and ties since his retirement (he was 51 at the time), but in this case, he would. We talked about the date and, to be honest, he did not make a great first impression in that initial phone conversation. He certainly wasn't using his Southern charm, which I eventually found out he had plenty of from North Carolina (go Tar Heels). He came to pick me up at my home, driving his black Mazda Miata and wearing a suit, and I admit I thought he was kind of cute. We went out with three other couples to this unusual event. I still have a picture of me trying on one of these red mink garments, which was really a mink-lined jacket with cuffs.

Worth had us all laughing, telling us his best jokes, and everyone thought he was funny and outgoing. I thought so, too. I didn't win a mink out of the 12 that were given away, but Worth did win a fur-covered police whistle and a teddy bear for me. If I had known I was going to marry him, I would have kept that whistle, but I gave it to a 12-year-old girl, who I thought would have more fun with it than I.

We enjoyed a great first date, but I boldly asked him if he wanted to have children, because I wasn't going to have a second date with anyone who didn't want children. He said he thought he could do that, but added that he was at a different place in life, which I don't think either of us understood. I was 40 and he was 51, and Worth had an eighteen-year-old son, Trey, from a prior marriage.

Three days later (Worth and I had already seen each other again), Dennis Vest, who had arranged our date, called Worth to inquire as to what he thought of me. Worth's response was that Dennis had messed up his life, because Worth thought he never wanted to be married again. One date had him reconsidering that vow!

Worth and I continued to date one another exclusively, and we were quite smitten with each another. As time went on and we had dated for ten months, I could tell for some reason he was pulling away from me. I had a hunch that he had changed his mind about having children, so I came out and simply asked him. He admitted that he didn't think he could handle having a baby at his age. I pondered what to do, but I had fallen in love with him. I did not want to lose him, so I trusted in God's will for our lives.

We had dated for 18 months when Worth invited me out to dinner and showed up in a suit! I was suspicious, and then he took me to the Top of the Triangle restaurant in downtown Pittsburgh, which is no longer around. He asked me to marry him during dinner, but in one breath he said, "Janet, I'd like to marry you as long as you're okay with not having children." I wasn't surprised because we had talked about it, and I knew his position had not changed.

There is no compromise between a husband and wife on an issue like children — both have to be in agreement. I felt in my heart that it would hinder what God could do in Worth's life if he stuck by his position of not wanting children. I have found it best to avoid those kinds of inner vows so as not to hinder what the Holy Spirit wants to do in anyone's heart.

But Worth had proposed and I loved him deeply, so I said "Yes," and promised I would not nag him about children. I did warn him, however, that I was going to pray for God to change his heart so that he would want children. That was the compromise we reached. He knew I would be praying, and I agreed not to have children. Truthfully, I was 40 at the time, so it wouldn't have been the best time to have children anyway. I am delighted to say that we have enjoyed a great marriage together — together facing every bend in the road.

In retrospect I realize my prayer to change Worth's heart was what led us to meet Olive in 1999, and here's how it happened. I developed a musical, *Lord, Make Me the Woman You Want Me to Be*, based on Mike Henning's prayers he had given me. I would tell others about those prayers, thinking they were just for me. People would come back six months later to tell me their lives had changed after they began praying *my* prayer. I was learning that God would honor those prayers of surrender no matter who prayed them, male or female.

We have a prayer loft in our home, which is a special place in my spiritual journey because that's where God so often speaks to me. One day, when I was praying there, God clearly said to me that I should ask Worth to make me a prayer kneeler for the loft. I went right downstairs to tell Worth of God's request of him to build me a kneeler. He asked how he was supposed to build it, and I told him it was up to him to decide. The only thing he said was, "Well, if God says I gotta, then I gotta!"

He took that task seriously, and the next day he left for the store to buy the materials to build it in accord with the drawings he spent time making. On the way, he stopped by my parents' home to say hello to my mom and dad. When he told them where he was going and his task, my mother, who was a pack rat, mentioned she happened to have a kneeler in her basement. Worth said, "No, God told Janet I have to build it, so I'd better build it." He left for the store and when he was halfway there, God told him it would be all right to use Mom's kneeler. He turned around and went back to get my mother's kneeler. Worth reupholstered it in a raspberry-colored fabric. We took it up to the prayer loft and put it under the window, where it still sits today. I'm still a little suspicious of whether God really told him Mom's kneeler was okay.

Early in our marriage, I was doing some performing when Worth challenged me to take my stage presence more seriously. I had unsuccessfully been trying to write a play and was praying about the show in my loft. I asked the Lord how to do a show because I wanted it to be totally for Him. One day, God answered my prayer and gave me the whole outline for the show in only about 30 minutes. I wrote down all the elements He wanted in it.

Then I sensed I was to call Rita Pinyot, who was the head of women's ministry at Christ Church of Grove Farm, to ask her if I could do my play during their Christmas show. I called her up, told her the story, and shared my sense that God wanted me to ask if I could do my first show there. I had already gone to Uganda with Christ Church's pastor, John Guest, and felt connected with him and his ministry, even though I wasn't a member. Rita said yes because I was a friend and she knew me from being a guest soloist in her church.

After Rita approved, she asked me to provide the

entertainment for an upcoming Christmas women's luncheon. I began to write the play and my friend, Eileen Hodgetts, who is a playwright herself, came along in the beginning to help me. She had also been the leader of many mission trips for ten years, so she identified with what I was trying to do.

She had been there in Uganda when I met Olive, so she knew the whole story and helped me tell it in the play. I performed it for the first time in December 2000, and from there we kept doing the show in the Eastern U.S., Africa, and many places in Pittsburgh, always with great responses from the audience. Eventually, I published a prayer journal to help people track their progress as God answered their prayers.

I was featuring the make-me-the-woman prayer in my play, teaching people how to use the prayer journal along with it. Then I started groups that took people through an eight-week cycle, during which we prayed that prayer together. We would meet weekly to go over what God did in us. The ladies were excited as they saw God making them the women He wanted them to be. They testified, among other things, how they were responding to adversity differently. I continued to pray with my friends from that time until 2006 when I began traveling more frequently to Uganda.

When Worth saw me perform, he was moved and touched. It was Worth who said to me he had seen many people perform on stage, but he had never seen any performer have such an emotional impact on an audience as I did. He told me I needed to be on the stage, because not doing so was a waste of talent. He decided to help me by becoming my agent.

His willingness to step in and do the work encouraged me, because it wasn't easy doing a Christian musical. I had always struggled with my self worth and I thought it so interesting that God gave me a man named Worth to help me realize that I had been sabotaging my life by only seeking men who were unworthy of who God wanted me to be. God gave me a man of great worth named Worth, who helped me increase my worth in my own eyes. I only know one other person named Worth, so there are not a lot of people running around with that name. I think it was God's plan, and also part of His sense of humor.

I was performing this play on the occasion I described in the Introduction. In the next chapter, I will tell you more about the play itself, how it developed, and how God used it in my life to change me and Worth as well. God was answering my prayers about children, and I didn't even know it.

Chapter 4

Worth and Olive

Worth and I were married in 1996, met Olive in Uganda in 1999, and I started performing my play in 2000. During those early years, Worth didn't really budge on the children issue. Even though I said I wouldn't be a nag (and I wasn't), it was still painful because I have strong mothering tendencies. I didn't want babies as much as I wanted to be a mother. I didn't pressure Worth, but I had a sadness and didn't know what to do next. I had no other course but to commit the entire thing to the Lord. Little did I know God would use Uganda and missions work to provide the breakthrough for which I had been praying.

In 1999, Eileen Hodgetts at Christ Church in Grove Farm led a trip to Uganda, and Worth and I went. Again I was praying that God would change Worth's heart. It was not our first time to Africa, for Worth and I had gone to Botswana in 1997 on a photo safari trip. When Worth said that he wanted to go to Botswana because the animals may not be there forever, we had only been married for two years. I said to him, "Africa? I haven't even gone to Hawaii yet!" When I thought of Africa, I kept thinking of Tarzan movies and of a place with gigantic spiders.

I said I would go as long as I could wear a safari outfit to look the part of a wild game hunter in our pictures. With that understanding we went, and we both fell in love with Africa. I enjoyed the sense of adventure we had when we went, and that sense is there on every trip. I have found nothing like it in all my travels.

I am serious when I said I connected with Africa on that trip. I did things I never thought I would do, like go down the Zambezi River in level four and five rapids. I took an ultralight plane over Victoria Falls, and I have never been so scared in my life. Those adventures opened my heart and creativity up to the wonders of Africa. They helped me to get rid of my fears and to see firsthand the beauty of the African continent. When we went to Uganda on the mission trip the next year, we wanted to connect with and help the people there.

We had discovered during our photo safari that it didn't take much money to change the lives of people there. During the safari, we went to the village of one of our guides. He had hollowed out his canoe and navigated us through the river delta among hippos, fish eagles and other wildlife. He took us to his village and all the little children gathered around us. Not many white people ever visit, and they were fascinated with us, studying our hands to see our veins and arteries because we have such a light complexion. I was captivated by those children, and God was preparing me for Uganda through that unplanned side excursion with our guide.

In 1999, on our first mission trip to Uganda with Pastor Guest and Eileen Hodgetts, we went to a remote town called Hoima to conduct an evangelistic crusade. The three-hour drive from the Entebbe airport was the only time in Africa where I was overwhelmed by the poverty of everyone. The children ran up to our car just to greet the team, and they were happy and smiling. I was not happy at all. It was the only time I wept and I tell you this because what I do today is not out of pity. I view those orphans as fellow human beings, and see how their lives could be different with just a little bit of help. I have tried to provide that help and go beyond money to set their hearts free.

All we had to conduct the crusade in Hoima was a megaphone and cheap sound system. Not much of a crowd had gathered while we were trying to hold the crusade in a field. It was then that we heard a noise from the people in the town square who were ignoring our little crusade. One of our friends went to scout out what was going on, and came back to report there there was a musical event going on, sponsored by Coca-Cola, which had a three-story-high stage with four or five thousand people listening to singers and watching dancers.

One of the men from our group approached the Coca-Cola planners and asked if we could use their stage when they were done. They agreed, which I have found to be quite African (they tend to be sharing people and are quite spontaneous). They charged us $150 to use their stage and sound equipment, so when they went off, we went on, and captured 4,000 people for our crusade. Talk about God's providence! We had practiced some songs and Worth was in a group of men who had all these praise songs ready to perform. Then John Guest preached. We were there for three hours and most of the people who were at the Coca-Cola concert stayed to listen.

While I was on stage singing, I saw Worth in the audience, holding a little boy in his arms the whole time. When I was finished, I went out into the audience and met the little boy whose name was Paul. Worth had quickly connected with that little boy, who was one of the children at a place called the Mustard Seed Baby's Home. As would happen, the next day, the team was going to visit that home.

That night after the Coca-Cola event, our team debriefed, and John Guest abruptly turned to Worth and said, "Why don't you adopt that little boy?" John Guest had no idea what Worth's position was on children, and I was sure Worth wasn't about to adopt that little boy. Something happened to Worth when he was holding that little boy, however, and John recognized it. Worth told me the next day that he didn't sleep all night because he was thinking about that boy. The next day, I went to the Mustard Seed Baby's Home with the team. It's a remarkable orphanage for all ages, even though they call it a baby's home. Worth did not go to the orphanage, but instead went to an all-day meeting with a group of people who were looking to help the Anglican diocese with various business ventures like a coffee farm. It was that day at the Mustard Seed Home when I met Olive.

Our truck pulled up and about 40 children came running to the vehicle, as is the case when visitors show up. I got out and Olive, who was seven at the time, came up and began talking to me. English is their official language, but not their native language. She showed me around and took me to her bedroom to see her bed. There were no other personal possessions or a place to even put them. She also showed me the office, which had a picture of all of the children along with her picture when she was eighteen months old and first came to the home. She was so engaging!

The children performed and sang, and Olive had a beautiful voice and was the lead singer. I could see that she was bright and we bonded at first sight. She stayed by my side the whole time, and I fell in love with that little girl. Paul, the little boy whom Worth had held, was there too, but I didn't have the connection with him that I did with Olive.

The next day was our last in Hoima, and it was a free day to do whatever we liked. I told Worth that he needed to come to the Mustard Seed to see Paul and also to meet Olive. He agreed, and that is where Worth first met Olive, and he was drawn to her right away, just as I had been. We saw her potential and beauty, but also realized the danger she was in if she stayed there as a little girl who is orphaned. They are always in danger due to being alone and having no one responsible to keep them safe.

When we were driving away, the children were all standing on a little knoll behind our vehicle and waving good bye. Worth and I started to weep, wondering what would happen to that little girl if she remained behind. The implications were something we didn't want to contemplate. As we left, Worth said that we should consider trying to adopt her. God had answered my prayer! I had not even considered adopting, but he was the first to speak the idea. Who would have thought the answer to my prayer would come in Africa? To this day, we still have a relationship with Paul. We helped him get his education because he was an important child in our journey. Paul captured our attention, but it was Olive who captured our hearts.

The church that founded the Mustard Seed Home was a church in Hopewell, PA called Prince of Peace. They had built the orphanage in 1994 after raising $25,000. When we came back home that September, somebody suggested calling a man named Bob Dwyer, who was in charge of a non-profit organization there that worked with Mustard Seed. When I called him, Bob informed me that Bishop John from Uganda happened to be in the States, and that maybe I could meet with him to find out about adopting. Bishop John did meet us at breakfast along with his wife, Harriet. I asked him if he thought it was a good idea to bring a child from their culture into our culture. He told me words I will never forget: "There's no substitute for daily love and care." He said we should not hesitate just because of cultural reasons.

Many significant spiritual moments in my life have been characterized by two things: praying and crying. I cried during breakfast when he said what he did. I didn't just cry, I started gushing water. Worth said that he thought a tsunami had hit at that moment. It truly was a watershed moment, so to speak.

We began the process for adoption in 1999. We spent that year doing everything we could to adopt. Then something remarkable and unusual took place. The wife of Uganda's president, Janet Museveni, was in the area to speak at a conference at LaRoche College. She came to Christ Church at Grove Farm one Sunday in the winter of 1999, where a reception was held in her honor. Pastor John Guest preached the sermon that day based on the story of the paraplegic whose friends dropped him down through the roof in front of Jesus. The emphasis of the service was that if there is something you want, you have to be proactive, seek it, and bring it right before Jesus.

Of course, I thought that Mrs. Museveni could help us with Olive, so at the reception I told her the story of how we met and fell in love with Olive, and were trying to adopt her. She invited me come with her to the Hilton Hotel in her limousine so we could talk about it. Worth followed in our car. Mrs. Museveni was kind and told us the laws in her country were difficult, and warned that there was nothing she could do about the laws. A family had to live in Uganda for three years, become a resident, and then apply to the courts for adoption.

She said she would help me, however, the same way she helped Maureen Reagan, President Reagan's daughter, to adopt a child. She promised to give me the name of the attorney who helped with that procedure, but reminded me that she couldn't guarantee anything, but was willing to advise us.

When Worth heard that, he didn't let grass grow under his feet. He obtained Maureen Reagan's number through friends in Pittsburgh who knew her. He called Maureen twenty-four hours later, and she gave us the information on how she was able to adopt. Maureen had met Rita, a Ugandan orphan, when she came to the States with a traveling group of orphans who were performing as a choir. Maureen did not have children either, and wanted the child to stay in America with her.

We started doing what we could, and in the summer of 2000, we felt we had a good chance of getting Olive through a student visa application. That was a bit of a stretch because she wasn't yet going to college. Instead, she was going to attend a Christian school here, but that's the route Maureen Reagan had followed.

Ugandan laws made it almost impossible to adopt. In fact, we tried to find anyone in the U.S. who had been able to adopt in Uganda, but couldn't find a single family. When it came time for anyone to petition the Ugandan courts for adoption, the judges were totally opposed to it. We heard of one couple who had lived there for three years. When they went to court, the judge requested that they sing fifteen songs in the language of the child they wanted to adopt. When he heard how well they sung them, he would make his ruling. They learned fifteen songs, but the judge didn't think they did a good enough job, so their request to adopt was denied.

We went to Uganda, but the adoption process was trying for both of us. Olive was able to get a passport, and everyone thought it was a sign that she was going to be able to come because she was only eight when she was approved. We were sure we would get her to the States because everyone seemed so positive about it in Uganda. We arrived that summer, thinking we had a good chance of this, but there was another major obstacle. Olive's mother and father were still alive; she was abandoned but not an orphan in the true sense of the word. We did now know this important fact until we were deep into the process — but we moved forward nonetheless.

Worth called the American consulate to set up an appointment. The consular officer told Worth he didn't care how much money he had or who he knew. All he cared about was seeing Olive's father and/or mother. When the consulate made that stipulation over the phone, it had not even been a consideration for us. Nobody knew where they were. We learned her mother was Rwandan and had left Olive when she was nine months old. The consulate official told us we had to go find one of them and not to bother coming back until we had.

We had spent a lot of time, money and effort to get to that point, and no one had ever told us we were going to need Olive's parents to be involved. We were disheartened and assumed this would never happen since no one knew where her parents were. We went to the orphanage and told them the story of how we needed to find her mother. The head of the orphanage said no one knew where she was, but one of the workers happened to overhear us talking, and told us to our delight that Olive's mother had just visited the day before. She had heard Olive was going to the United States and wanted to say goodbye. No one had told the head of the orphanage.

Since her mother, whose name is Viata, had been in Hoima the day before, we hoped to track her down before she left and take her to the consulate. Olive's aunt had put her in the orphanage when her father couldn't raise her any longer. (It's almost impossible for a man to raise a child in that culture for many reasons). Both parents had problems with alcohol, which was one of the reasons why they couldn't raise their six children

We tracked down the aunt and, through various people, found out the mother was probably staying in the bush in a relative's hut. We drove out to the village and, lo and behold, there she was! We asked if she would go with us to Kampala to go to the U.S. embassy to help us bring Olive to America, and she agreed to do so. One of the missionaries who went with us tried to hug her, but she shrank back. Olive's mother was a Tutsi refugee from the Rwandan genocide, and she was probably protecting herself more than refusing to receive our love.

The next day we went to Kampala, the capital of Uganda. It was a type of pilgrimage where the act of going was more important than the outcome. That car ride was remarkable for Olive. She had never been out of Hoima, and that day she was in a vehicle with the people who had all been instrumental in her life: her mother who gave birth to her but then abandoned her; her aunt who saved her and took her to the orphanage; the head of the orphanage who had raised her from the time she was eighteen months old and taught her about Jesus; and Worth and I, who were trying to adopt her.

We sat in the back of the vehicle because Olive was afraid to be in the vehicle with her mother. She didn't fully grasp what was happening, regardless of what we told her. She thought her mother was going to take her away. She sat between Worth and me, holding our hands, the entire trip to Kampala, which was about a four-hour ride. It wasn't an easy ride then, but the roads are better now.

Before we went to the embassy, we tried to prepare Olive's mother for what they would be asking her. She didn't speak English so the aunt served as translator. We were coaching the mother to pretend that she had a loving bond with Olive and to say that she had abandoned her due to the terrible circumstances. We were applying for a student visa, and we wanted the officials to know that we intended for Olive to come back to Uganda one day.

When we arrived, the officials took her and her mother into a private room without us. To make a long story short, they ended up denying the application for

Olive's visa. It was obvious there wasn't any relationship between Olive and her mom, but they still turned us down.

At that point, I was devastated because I really believed it was going to go through. After all, we had found her mother and everything was lining up. After the ruling, I sat down on the rocks outside the embassy, where I released through my tears all of the frustration and discouragement in me. We were all there, and the mother too, and the Ugandan guards who worked for the embassy saw us and didn't know what to make of this unusual scene.

All of a sudden Evace, the head of the orphanage, jumped up and told me to stop crying and start worshipping, loudly began preaching about how Jesus Christ had risen from the dead. She went on and I somehow came to my senses, realizing she was correct. In the meantime, Olive sat down on the curb and drew a picture, which I think was the way she envisioned what an American house looked like. It was a square house with a big sun shining in the sky. Happy flowers lined the front of the house. It was her way of saying that one day she would come to our house; she was not sad. Somehow she knew it would come true, and it did in 2012.

We went out to eat at a chicken and fries place, and then drove Olive back to the orphanage. Her mother, I believe, moved to Uganda with her husband after that. I saw the mother again in 2012, so Olive could say good-bye before she came to the States. Her father, Emmanuel, died from disease in the fall of 2015.

Before I tell you what we did after this setback, I want to share something with you that I did not find out until 2012 when Olive and I were flying to the States for her to go to school here. I had never given much thought as to why Olive and I connected so quickly when I met her the day the team first visited the Mustard Seed Home. A few months before we came, Olive was afraid because the orphanage leaders had told her that they were going to resettle her with her father. They needed the room to house more babies. Olive told me that she was crying out to God every night that someone would save her, so she wouldn't have to go back to her father.

One of the workers noticed her crying and asked what she was crying about. Olive told her, and the worker promised to pray with Olive that something would happen so they wouldn't have to send her back to her father. They delayed sending her back because the Home heard that an American missionary group was coming. Since Olive was the head of the praise team, she had to stay to sing.

The morning that we were coming, Olive was praying by her bed and God directed her to go to the woman who had no candy. Our team got out of the vehicle and Olive came looking for the woman who had no candy to give out, and that woman was me. She was so remarkable and engaging in the way she came right up to me. It never occurred to me why she chose me, and Olive never told me because she never thought it was that important. To me, however, it was enlightening because that was why I bonded with her so quickly – two souls meant to meet that day.

After the denial, however, Worth and I still believed Olive was to be part of our lives. We didn't know what that would look like, but we were not going to abandon her. Now let's move on to what happened next, for God had changed Worth's heart, and we were not about to turn back now.

Chapter 5

Kinship Kids

For obvious reasons, 2001 was a trying year, and I was in deep depression after things didn't work out to adopt Olive in the previous year. God had changed Worth's heart, which I thought was the biggest hurdle to clear, and then it looked like it wasn't going to work out to have a child after all. We were left with one important question: What should we do now? In that year, we were trying to figure out what to do, looking at different options because we hadn't given up on the idea of adoption. We went back to Uganda in 2001 with a group called Encounter Uganda.

The two-year struggle to figure out a way to adopt Olive had taken a toll on all of us. There was no clear direction yet. The week before we were going back to Uganda with Encounter Uganda, I told Worth that we had to do something so we could carry some good news with us. We decided to find a boarding school in Uganda where Olive could get a good education. That way, if she ever came to the U.S., she wouldn't be so far behind her peers. Our impression was that her educational options weren't good in the village, and it was common for Ugandan children to go away for school, even at a young age.

The Encounter Uganda team came to our house for a going-away gathering, and they invited Sylvia Tamusuza to come tell us about the culture there. Sylvia was attending the University of Pittsburgh at the time, and was going back to Uganda the following week, having completed her doctorate in ethnomusicology in four years. The timing was perfect for her to be at our house. After this amazing time learning about the culture in Uganda while being entertained by her, Worth and I pulled her aside to ask if she had a recommendation for a boarding school in Uganda, since she was a professor.

She asked what we would do with Olive when she was on school breaks. Without other options, we assumed she would go back to the orphanage. Sylvia told us to come see her the next day, which would give her time to pray about how she would answer our question. We went to see her at her dorm room at the University of Pittsburgh the next day, and Sylvia offered to be Olive's mother in Uganda right on the spot! I once again saw God's hand in this, because if I had not suggested that we try to put her in a boarding school, we would not have asked Sylvia about it. Sylvia returned to Uganda that next week and, by the end of 2001, had taken Olive into her home at the end of that school year. Olive lived with her, her husband Justinian and their children through her high school years.

During that trip in 2001, Eileen's husband, Graham Hodgetts, was with us. He made a great suggestion that we have a public ceremony to make Olive our spiritual daughter. We thought and prayed about that, and felt it was a good idea for several reasons. First, it would make it clear in Olive's mind that we were serious about her being part of our family. Second, it was beneficial for us to solidify our commitment to this child. Third, it was good for the Ugandans to be exposed to the concept of spiritual adoption, which was still not part of their cultural fabric. We asked the bishop, Wilson Teremanyua, to lead the ceremony, which was attended by about 100 people.

It was a remarkable event and it did solidify in Olive's mind that we were part of her life for good. That's quite an important step for orphans who are not accustomed to stable, ongoing relationships in their lives. In fact, when we visited her the following year, Olive said to me, "Mommy, if you ever forget me, the devil will get you because of the words you promised." I was surprised, but on some level I knew she was right. We had made a vow before God to be there for her.

One of the objectives of Orphaned Heart Ministries is to educate Ugandans about the benefits of committing to be spiritual parents to their orphans. Those children need to hear someone publicly say they will commit to love them for the rest of their lives. That should also be a role the church helps fill — to offer re-parenting services for those who are without parents. Our ceremony was the first I had heard of, but I can see how important it can be to many orphaned children so that they feel that kind of tangible love. We went back to the U.S. without Olive, but God was using our disappointment to create a new type of what we call "kinship relationship" with her and eventually with others.

We returned to Uganda regularly where Worth

helped establish a coffee farm to provide jobs and revenue. The coffee is shipped to the U.S., roasted here, and then marketed under the label *Ugandan Gold*. Today, it is a beautiful coffee plantation in Uganda with 37 acres and thousands of trees. The U.S. Ambassador came to visit once and said it was the finest farm he had seen in Uganda! That farm gave us more reasons to go back so we could stay involved in Olive's life.

Keep in mind that there was a social crisis going on at this time. The AIDS pandemic had created many orphaned children, 2.5 million in Uganda alone. There were few systems in place to deal with the crisis, and many tried to ignore it. There are too many children to ignore, however. We saw a chance to help not only Olive, but also many other children in desperate need.

Sylvia and I knew that God had brought the three of us together – Sylvia, Olive and me – for a greater purpose. We had developed a model with Sylvia being Olive's "mother" on the ground. We wanted to use this model to help other children. The model involved finding an American to sponsor a child's care and education, while an African family would care for that child so they had a safe home and loving family in their homeland.

Hence, we adopted the name the Olive Kinship Program for the ministry, which was similar to the foster child program in the U.S. We expanded the program to go beyond orphanages as we identified Ugandan families who would take in to their homes our kinship kids. Those children were not actually orphans who had lost their parents, but were being raised by an aunt or grandfather who needed financial help with raising them.

My mom and dad believed in and supported our

mission work in Uganda. Toward the end of his life, my dad was sick with a treatable case of thymus gland cancer. The disease that finally took his life, however, was Alzheimer's. He stopped eating, and contracted pneumonia. I often took him to the doctor with my mother, and one day after a visit, we had lunch at an outdoor restaurant. At this point, I had stopped sharing much information with him about what I was doing in Uganda because he wasn't well.

At lunch, however, I began telling him about my most recent trip and how I had visited schools for the kinship program in Hoima, Uganda. I described the scene of being in a classroom where there were 150 students, one teacher and only one set of books. I reported that the children had to stand on their desks in an attempt to see the book that the teacher was using.

As I told him of the conditions in the school, he started to weep. I had never seen my father weep, but he started crying and asked me to stop because he couldn't take what I was telling him. It was breaking his heart to hear what orphans and children had to deal with in Uganda.

He told me that I had to tell people about this situation, and even suggested I write a book to share the story. What's more, he said he wanted to help me. He added that people had to know what was going on with the children, and I was the one to tell them. He was getting worked up and I was getting concerned for his health. I said, "Dad, you aren't feeling well. Let's wait until your treatment is over and then we will talk about how you can help." He kept repeating that it was urgent to tell their story so we could help those kids. He died shortly after that in October of 2004.

I don't remember when my dad ever told me that he loved me. Six months earlier, I had spent some time journaling about that very issue. By this time, prayer journaling was a vital part of my walk and relationship with the Lord. It was helpful to track my progress and to pay attention to new prayers God was showing me. In my journal, I told the Lord that I knew my father loved me, but he had never said it, and I needed to hear him say it. That was my need, and I wondered if my father needed it, too. While I was journaling, I felt the Holy Spirit indicate that my father would tell me he loved me before he died. I immediately wrote that down. Shortly thereafter, my father had a heart attack due to the pneumonia and other physical problems he was battling.

After his heart attack, my mother, brother, sister and I were in the hospital together. We had all prayed as a family and felt he should have a respirator. Dad was conscious as the doctors installed the respirator. While he was there in a critical care unit, my mother knew he was angry with her because he wasn't looking at her. It turns out he had stipulated in his will that he did not want to be kept on life support.

He was on the respirator for two days when Mother said she wanted to take it out because it wasn't what he wanted. She could tell it upset him to have it, and she didn't want their relationship to end that way. When Pastor John and Kathie Guest came to visit, we asked how to go about removing a respirator in a thoughtful way. He suggested we make a prayer service and plan it when everyone was there so they could say goodbye to him before we removed it.

Pastor John and his wife came back the next day,

which was a Sunday. They prayed and we took the respirator out, and had two hours with my dad in the critical care unit. My brother was there with his wife, along with their two twin daughters, Leah and Anna, who were just one-month old. Dad got to hold them. My sister was there with her two adult children, Stephanie and James, along with Worth and me. I sang the Lord's Prayer at his bedside and people talked to him about how important he was to everybody and what a great dad he was. Since the respirator was out, he could talk a little bit. Then his breathing started to become more labored. Then he pointed to each of us and said, "I love you." He said that to each one of us, he said it to me, and then died, just like I had written in my prayer journal six months earlier.

He said what I wanted to hear to all of us in our family before he died. The next morning, I woke up at 5 AM with a start and could hear my dad's voice. I know he was a Christian and went to heaven, but all I can say is I heard his voice. I heard him say to give the money from the funeral to the orphans to fulfill the conversation he had with me in the restaurant. My brother and sister agreed, and my mother also thought it was a good idea.

The week before, I had joined the board of directors for Love and Care Family International, and we had discussed expanding our outreach to include the kinship program. In Dad's obituary, we requested that money be donated to the Love and Care Family project in his memory. People gave about $3,500, and that is what started the kinship program. Now I am following through on writing the book to let people know about the orphan dilemma in Africa, just as Dad had directed me to do. I know he would have been one of my greatest cheerleaders.

Whenever we went back to Uganda, I continued performing my one-woman show. Sylvia first started caring for Olive in 2001 through Love and Care Family International, but it was in 2006 when I performed the show that fell apart, that Orphaned Heart Ministries was born. When I was humiliated during that show, the Holy Spirit moved and I knew Sylvia was right — people did not understand adoption and the orphan dilemma or how they were suffering from a spirit of abandonment and rejection.

After the re-parenting ceremony with Olive to help her have a sense that someone would be there for her even though her parents were absent from her life, we began to wonder why more Africans didn't take to the concept of adoption. What was preventing Africans from taking in children? We knew some of the horrible things that happened after parents died with the extended families, how the aunts and uncles would evict the orphaned children from the house. If the orphans did stay, they were often the last to get food or other necessities. If there was any government help for those families, they often diverted it from the orphan and gave it to their own children.

One of the other interesting things that emerged from the 2006 trip was our sponsorship of a workshop that focused on the issue of adoption for local workers and leaders, and about 60 people attended the event. We invited Ugandan experts to highlight for attendees what people were doing in Africa to adopt and care for children. It turned out to be an amazing conference attended by the heads of orphanages and various agencies, social workers, and government officials.

Sylvia brought forth the example of Jane and Jonah, siblings she knew from her neighborhood. There were

10 orphans from one mother and father who died from AIDS. Immediately the aunts and uncles were trying to get the children to leave because they had legal right over the house. If there had been some sort of adoption process in place, it would have been so much better for the children. We had some wonderful people who took in foster children, but those foster parents didn't have any legal relationship with the child. If those foster parents passed away or something happened to them, those kinship kids would immediately be asked to leave the house. We wanted some kind of legal security for the kid's future, and that is why we held that conference to raise awareness within Uganda to the benefits of Africans adopting orphans for whom they cared.

People at the conference were all saying how confusing the adoption process was. At one point during the conference, one government official spoke who seemed to know everything about how to adopt in Africa. He held up a form and said it was the one needed to get the adoption process started. Everyone present said they had never seen that form before. That highlighted the problem that even the most experienced professionals in the industry didn't know where to go or how to start the adoption process. When we asked him how people could find out how to do this kind of thing in Uganda, he told us they at one time had a radio program that distributed this information to the public, but the funding had dried up and the show was no longer on the air.

Sylvia and I expanded our kinship program, and we prayerfully asked God to bring us children of His choosing. I was attending Trinity Seminary in Ambridge, PA, where I met Reverend Sam Opal. Sam told me the story of his brother who died in an automobile accident. His brother had 11 children from three wives. Sam was responsible to educate the surviving children, but he didn't have the funds since he struggling with his own kids. We had just started the kinship program, so I asked him for more information on the younger children, since Americans are more prone to open their hearts for the younger kids as opposed to the older ones.

Sam's deceased brother had twin daughters who were ten years old and their mother's name was Frances. We took those two girls into the program as our first kinship kids after Olive. Sylvia did not know these children, but God brought them across our path. The twins continued to live with their mother during school breaks, but lived in boarding school when the term was in session. We found sponsors in the States to pay for their boarding school fees. We started helping them in 2003 and now they are in college, excelling in their work, and have hope for a good future.

Another example was closer to home for Sylvia. She had neighbors and the mother and father died from AIDS and also had 11 children to multiple wives. Sylvia heard that the aunts and uncles were trying to remove the children from their house. Sylvia began working to help them stay in their house. But two children, Jane and Jonathan, the youngest from that family, became part of the kinship program. We took them in, found a home for them, and they have been involved with the program. As of this writing, we have 12 children in the Kinship Program. It's not big, but it keeps Sylvia and me involved in helping orphans. Over the years, I have learned more about Sylvia's story while staying in touch with the needs of orphans through our kinship model.

I have recently talked with some Americans who have served as foster parents. Children have the same heart everywhere – to be loved and give love in a situation of safety and stability. Here in the U.S., there is a huge societal problem. The government pays foster parents to take in at-risk children. When the children reach the age of 18, however, the money is cut off to those foster parents. Some foster parents are only motivated by money to take in children, so when there is no more money, many foster kids are left to fend for themselves.

This only reinforces the Orphaned Heart in children when they are left without a home. Again, in my kinship program in Africa, Sylvia and I strive to give the children the sense that they will always have a home to come to with a stable family they can connect with as they mature into adults.

Over time, Sylvia has embraced these kinship kid, and when they're on break from school and it's too hard for them to get back home, she has them stay at the Miriam Duggan home, the home founded by several churches in the Pittsburgh area. There they have some interaction with younger children and with some adult care under Sylvia's oversight.

I hope you see how God brought so much good out of the trauma of our failed adoption process. Sylvia took Olive in when Olive was not attending boarding school, and they became our first kinship family. Failure to adopt Olive caused us to learn more about the orphan problem and the laws and cultural mores that prevented orphan care. That led us to expand the kinship program to what it is today through Sylvia, families in the U.S. who provide support for the children in Uganda, and the kinship families in Uganda.

When we could not adopt Olive, we had our local ceremony to commit to her care. Bishop Wilson created a ceremony by adjusting the marriage ceremony in the Anglican prayer book and adapting it to spirituall adopt a child.

This certainly took care of many practical issues concerning the orphan problem, but it did not deal with root issues, especially of what being an orphan did to a child's heart. We had begun Orphaned Heart Ministries, but now it was time to really deal with deeper issues that would lead to the orphan's freedom from despair and rejection. Let's look at our continuing journey to find real, lasting solutions to this endemic problem.

SECTION TWO

•

GETTING TO THE ROOT OF THE PROBLEM

Chapter 6

Searching for
an Answer

I have visited East Africa almost every year since I made my first visit in 1999, except for 2004 when my father passed away. Yet, when you commit to ministry, life doesn't stop, and you have to learn to manage life at home and life overseas. In 2005, seven months after my dad died, Worth started having chest pains one morning as we were getting ready to go to church. It turned out that he was having a heart attack. His treatment was as routine as treating the heart can be, and there was no heart damage. About a week later, he woke me up at 5 AM. He said he was trying to wait until later in the day to disturb me, but he had been bleeding in the throat for several hours. He felt he should go to the hospital emergency room, so we quickly made our way there.

When we got there, Worth best described the sensation that his throat had become a factory for blood clots. He didn't have any pain, but they kept coming and coming. His tongue was a conveyer belt and was just churning them out. The doctor walked in, looked at him, and exclaimed in amazement, "What the hell?" All of that is to say it was a weird situation. They kept him in the hospital for three days. I was thinking it had to do with his heart, since he had just had a heart attack. Without a clear answer, the doctors finally decided to cauterize his throat, because they didn't know what to do to stop the bleeding. They performed that procedure and recommended that he have his throat examined, and he was released. Unfortunately, Worth put off going to the specialist.

We attended my stepson Trey's wedding in April. As we were leaving, Trey, who is truly like a son to me, gave us a gift of a painting depicting the arms of Jesus coming out of a lighthouse surrounded by tumultuous waves. That picture was fixed in my mind after only seeing a photocopy of the picture, which Trey was going to give to us later. We came home and Worth finally went in to see the doctor. While I was in the waiting room, a woman next to me was crying, so I felt that I should minister to her. I read her the Bible verse about not being afraid because God has provided for all of us in the past and He will take care of us in the future. Little did I know I was preaching to myself.

Just as I finished praying with her, the doctor came out and wanted to talk with me. She took me in the conference room and said, with a gigantic smile on her face (I am still not sure of the reason for that), that Worth had throat cancer. I was shocked. She said that she suspected he had not told me, so she wanted to have a private time with me. It was true; he hadn't breathed a word, not giving me any indication of the doctor's suspicion. The doctor informed me that Worth had an eight-centimeter tumor in the wall of his throat.

We went home and I felt like the ground had been pulled out from under me. Worth was obviously concerned, but was calm. That day, we got a copy of the *Pittsburgh Magazine* in the mail, and it listed the top doctors in Pittsburgh, and one of them was the doctor who diagnosed Worth that day, whose name was Jennifer Grandis. It made me feel that whatever happened, she was a top doctor in her field for throat issues. God gave me some peace.

I kept thinking of that painting, seeing Jesus with His arms outspread, and it gave me reassurance that Jesus was with us in the midst of the storm. It was a large tumor, but they caught it right above stage three. The doctor felt they could deal with it without an operation, using radiation and chemotherapy. Worth never smoked, drank much or participated in any of the potential causes for that kind of cancer.

It's interesting that we would have never known about the cancer without the heart attack. When they increased his blood thinners after the heart attack, it made the area of the cancer bleed profusely. God, in His mercy, used his minor heart attack to expose the more insidious cancer tumor. I thank God to this day that his cancer was found so early.

The day after we discovered Worth had cancer, Dr. Sam Annankra from Ghana came to stay with us. Sam was also fighting cancer and was back in Pittsburgh for a follow-up examination. God had Sam there for us at that time. He informed us that he had prayed the entire day about what to say concerning the ordeal we were facing.

He advised us to keep claiming Worth's healing. Then he drew a picture of a plane going through the clouds. Sam explained that the clouds are what we see from Earth, but once we get above the clouds, we see the beauty.

He said that when we seek healing, we have to go beyond what the doctors are saying, although we still listen to what they have to say. He told us that we had to keep in mind that there is another realm, the heavenly one. We took Sam's advice during the sobering two months of Worth's treatment. Worth was quite sick a couple of times, but he got a clean bill of health afterwards, and it was remarkable how he handled it, too. Every Saturday, no matter how he felt, he crawled to the computer and wrote an account of what he was going through. I called these writings his epistles. He did that every Saturday, just to let everyone know what he was going through, and many who read his accounts were inspired by his steadfastness. That was how we spent 2005.

Our friend Dr. Sam passed away in 2007 from hepatitis, which he had contracted ten years earlier. He was a pediatrician, a colonel in the air force, and an evangelist. He stayed with us on and off for about 18 months during his cancer treatments. During that time, I saw the spiritual disciplines that undergirded the person he was. He was a public figure, but his personal disciplines were strong and formidable. He was a great person to have in my life. In 2006, I went back to Uganda. While Worth was going through treatments, I continued working with Love and Care, mostly assisting with the practical aspects of how to help the kinship program.

When I came back from my trip that included the show with the problems in 2006, I was convicted by God of the spirit of abandonment and rejection that Sylvia had mentioned, and I had seen firsthand the spiritual diseases destroying the lives of the African people. I was determined to discover a formula or remedy I could take back with me to Uganda, for it held the key for those children to live full lives.

There were legal and cultural problems that were creating problems for the children, but the real problem was on a spiritual level where they suffered from a spirit of rejection and abandonment. That quest led me in 2008 to an inner healing prayer conference in Seattle conducted by Rita Bennett. The question I had that only God could answer was this: How can a person be healed from these wounds? As I sat through those conference sessions, I recognized right away that I had discovered where the people in Africa needed to heal, and that was at the emotional level where their memories lived. It was in Seattle that I first learned about inner healing prayer, and then also sat under training by Judith MacNutt here locally at the Lazarus Center.

I had been going to Trinity School for Ministry in Ambridge, Pennsylvania on a part-time basis, enjoying taking classes but without any specific goal. In 2008, after my experience in Seattle under Rita Bennett, I got a burning desire to return to Uganda to bring this healing power to address the spirit of rejection and abandonment.

I needed the theological training from Trinity as a foundation to go to the church and beyond. Therefore, I decided to turn my credits into completing a Master of Arts Degree in Missions. I completed my degree in May of 2012. My last three credits were an independent study under the supervision of Dr. Grant LeMarquand, and my topic was "Healing the Orphaned Heart in East Africa." I praise God for the knowledge He gave me. Eventually, I stopped performing my show, because I found that teaching and doing hands-on ministry were much more effective.

While at Trinity, I met someone from Kenya who became an important person to help me refocus my work in Africa. In 2008, a man I didn't know named Qampicha (pronounced Kam-PEE-cha) Daniel Wario approached me in the campus bookstore during a five-minute class break. He mentioned that he would like to tell me about his people in northern Kenya and how difficult their life was due to poverty, lack of water, and the nomadic life of their herdsmen trade. He explained that it was difficult for Christians to come together for training, teaching, or evangelism because they were so scattered and beleaguered. Qampicha desired to bring the Christians together at a place where they could congregate, learn more about Scripture, and be trained. He had a big heart to equip his people for successful living. In the few minutes we had together, he also explained that the children needed to be taught because they did not possess a Christian worldview.

I listened politely, but I was only a part-time student who had a passion for Uganda, not Kenya. In addition to school, my mom became sick with cancer in 2009. Worth was still working on the *Uganda Gold* project, and we were still supporting Olive while working with Sylvia. We were delighted that Olive was able to come to the U.S. with Sylvia for a visit in January of 2009. Since Sylvia was her legal guardian, the Ugandan officials were not worried she would try to stay here in the States and granted her a visitor's visa. They were here for one month, but it was a difficult month for us as a couple.

In January 2002, Worth had invested a significant portion of his cash with an investment company in Florida. He had done due diligence on the managers, everything except hiring a private detective, and felt good about them. But seven years later, in January of 2009, he was informed by the man's office that the head of the firm had fled and all of the money was gone. Of course, we were devastated, Worth more than I, because he had officially retired. He had a good pension, Social Security, and a fair amount of 401(k) money, but the lost funds represented about 32% of his net worth. I wasn't working too much either since I was attending to my studies, but I was selling some insurance on the side.

Now you can understand why that January was so trying. Olive was here for the first time, we had financial concerns, and the three of us were driving together to Florida for a previously-planned holiday. We stopped at the home of an Anglican priest named Mike Messina in Ocala, Florida, because I wanted him to pray for Olive. Worth was in a depressed emotional state and not himself when we stopped for prayer. Reverend Mike had two intercessors with him who were praying for Olive.

When Olive first arrived in the U.S., she was filled with anger and mistrust from all that had happened in her life. She found it difficult to express her feelings and receive our love. Of course, this was due to many traumatic experiences she had encountered, which is part of her story and will not be included here.

While we were praying, I looked at Worth who was sitting in a high-back black chair, and he looked so defeated and diminished as a man. I saw how his identity of himself was partially attributable to his financial success, and to have a setback like that had affected his concept of who he was. Mike asked Worth if he wanted prayer and Worth agreed, so Father Mike prayed. It turned out to be an important event for Worth, as I will explain later.

As if all that wasn't enough, when we got back in the car, we received a call when we were a half an hour from my mom's place in Stuart, Florida. Mom had fallen and broken her leg! She had to be hospitalized, and I wasn't sure if we were all going to make that vacation happen. I am not sure what Olive thought about life in America at that point.

While watching the national news, we found out that the FBI was looking for the man who absconded with Worth's money. After two weeks, he turned himself in and went to jail. It was a tragic event for many people like Worth who had trusted that man and invested so much. Worth was deeply concerned all the while we were in Florida, saying that we needed to reevaluate our situation, consider downsizing our home, and scaling back our lifestyle. My 84-year-old mother was confined to a rehabilitation center for three months with a non-weightbearing cast since they could not operate and put pins in her leg at her age. She had to stay off her foot, which meant she had to remain in Florida for three months and could not return to Pittsburgh.

We stayed in Florida for those three months and it was the Lord's doing, although at first we did not realize it. If we had returned to Pittsburgh, we may have overreacted to our loss. Instead, we stayed in Florida where we had a chance to pray and reflect. The word that kept coming to us during that time was *restoration*. We didn't necessarily believe it was restoration financially, but restoration concerning how we viewed ourselves as capable, good people. We were praying for that and for my mother. When we flew back home in April, we got word that my mother had been diagnosed with a grapefruit-sized intestinal tumor and was given three months to live. I volunteered to deliver the news to her myself.

I informed Mom that the reason she couldn't eat was because she had an inoperable tumor. She knew the Lord, and we were willing to accept whatever decision she made about receiving treatment or not, because all of us knew where she was going when she died. After I told her, she nodded her head and said it was okay, God was preparing her because she had been having dreams of heaven. The night before I told her, she had a dream that Jesus was carrying her through pink and blue clouds. She asked where He was taking her and His answer was, "You'll know soon, my daughter." Mom said she would be fine and she was. In fact, she threw a "Celebration of Life" party, not to say goodbye to the people who were there, but to see all of the people she loved – or perhaps more accurately for them to see her.

There were 150 people at the party. When they arrived, they found her sitting in a chair, so a receiving line naturally formed to greet her, and people described it as like coming to a wake where the person was sitting at the end of the line – alive rather than in a casket. Many people were crying the whole time, yet she had an amazing countenance of love for everyone. Pastor John Guest was there, gave an evangelistic call, and three people gave their lives to Christ. At the end of the evening, she danced to my father's favorite song, as the remaining 45 people made a circle and took turns dancing with her. And that's where I did my grieving for her through dancing and singing with her. The song was *Long Ago and Far Away*.

She died in July about six weeks later on our wedding anniversary. In both local papers, there was an article about her going-away party and how she handled the end of her life as a woman of faith. About a month after her death, I get a call from my attorney telling me that my mother had left me money that amounted to about three times more than we had lost. It did not escape our notice that with one phone call we lost it all and with one phone call we got it all back. It was clear that God was saying it was His money. (By the way, Worth has since recovered more than half of the money out of which he was swindled!)

I donated some of that money to start a school in Kenya under the oversight of Qampicha, and some of it to pay my own way as I continue to travel to East Africa to teach people how to be free. I have a ministry that accepts donations, for what I am doing is more than I can finance. My purpose in relating this story is to show how God restored our money so we would have the resources necessary to do His work in Africa.

But now, let me finish the story of Qampicha, the Kenyan pastor I met at school in the bookstore. When we first started talking in 2008, I didn't have any money to help him. In 2010, he was graduating, and our schedules were never in sync, so I didn't see him often. When I did see him across campus, however, the conversation in the bookstore would come back to me. I would always tell myself that I needed to get with him and talk about his people in Kenya. The sense that we needed to talk kept growing, so finally I made a special effort to find him, since I knew he was ready to graduate. Finally, I found him and asked if he remembered our conversation almost two years earlier. Before he responded, he asked for me to give him a moment to compose himself because he couldn't speak.

Tears streamed down his face and he said he had been thinking of the conversation every time he saw me for the past year and a half. He did not pursue talking to me further because he didn't want to bother me. When I finally approached him, he said it was the greatest affirmation he had ever had in his ministry, which truly shocked me. He also knew that we were supposed to talk, and the longer he waited, the more that urgency grew in him as it had in me. God was obviously working in both of us.

We agreed to have dinner where we could talk about what it would take to help his people. He said a Christian primary school was the most urgent need to give children a good education along with more knowledge of the Bible. Qampicha lives in a north Kenyan town called Sololo, near the Ethiopian border where the residents are 85% Muslim. The reason he responded so emotionally when I approached him was that he has just been telling God that he didn't want to go back to Kenya with nothing but the Gospel, even though it's the one thing that would truly free and save his people.

He knew his people needed something tangible to supplement the Gospel, because they needed things to survive this life and not simply prepare for the next one. He and his friends were praying, asking God if Qampicha should even go back home to this desolate area without some kind of practical help. Then on that fateful day when I approached him, Qampicha felt that he had the answer to his prayers. I decided to be part of the answer to his prayer to help him with a school. Before he left for home, we met with a dozen other friends he had made at Trinity to talk about building a school. We formed what is called the Kenya Christian Education Partnership (KCEP), and some of the money my mother left me helped begin the project.

Like other events in my life, I look back now and thought I was going to a simple meeting to talk to a pastor from Kenya, but it turned out to be so much more. We didn't know we were going to start a school until we all met. Every one of the people who began the project are now in different states working in a variety of churches. They have all helped fund the building of a school through various sponsorships, and we have stayed close and connected in our passion for the children of Kenya

At first, we put together our bylaws and laid out a capital campaign for the building program in Sololo. The mission we originally planned was bigger than one school building – it was to help build other schools in northern Kenya one at a time. We are just finishing up the school in Sololo, so we will see what God has in store for us after this. We have built a school with eight grades, which is the equivalent of our elementary and middle school here in the States. Our guiding Bible verse for the school is John 21:14, where Jesus responds to Peter that if he loves him, Peter should feed His lambs.

We raised about $50,000 during the first year, and started building the Primary Phase One and the nursery. My brother, sister, and I gave money for the nursery in my parent's name. Then Bob Moran, a dear friend to Worth and me, contributed to build the first grade or Primary

Phase One in honor of his deceased wife. They started building in December and a team from Trinity School for Ministry (including myself, Canon Dr. Rev. John Macdonald and Rev. Amanda Goin Burgess) arrived for a visit the first week of January. We saw the two completed classroom buildings and the children at their desks with new uniforms. It was remarkable to see and one of the most fulfilling moments of my life.

A local committee was appointed to form an operational board of directors for the school, and they made a decision to name the school Tumaini. In Kiswahili, the local language, Tumaini means "hope." I cannot think of a more appropriate name for this institution of learning than the "hope" it gives to each of the 480 students and their entire community.

One of the things the school does is to provide something I can see, touch and feel. Some ministries focus their efforts on developing people, and of course, people are always developing and growing. When a building is finished, however, you can see the progress of your investment right away. In God's purpose for me, He's given me two ministries. KCEP produces tangible results that I can see and appreciate right away. When that school complex is completed, the job of building the school will be done.

Yet KCEP will also have an ongoing aspect to our ministry, for the children there will need sponsors to help pay for their education. I will see the buildings complete, but the work with the children will be ongoing, just like my work with Orphaned Heart Ministries. As I write, we have received funding from the Anglican Relief and Development Fund to complete the Sololo school project by building our two largest buildings: the multipurpose building and the administrative block.

I visited Sololo in 2011 and again in the summer of 2014. As I told you, the first year we built the two classrooms. Then in the spring, we began construction on a water tank along with classrooms for Primary grades 2 and 3, which were completed in January 2011. Then in 2012, we built Primary 4, with the objective of completing one classroom every year, up through grade eight. The final two classrooms, P-7 and P-8, were finished in December of 2015. In each year, our goal was to build one additional classroom.

When I finished my Master's degree, I was ready to resume my quest to bring ministry for the Orphaned Heart to Uganda, thinking I could devote all the time I had invested in my studies to my ministry. Little did I know that more opposition was just ahead, which you will find out about in the next chapter.

Chapter 7

Healing Conferences in Uganda

From the beginning, a man named Simon Peter Dembe has helped lead the Orphaned Heart Ministries in Uganda. Simon's father died from AIDS when he was four, and his mother died when he was seven. Sylvia raised him, but he spent a lot of time on the streets. He has a remarkable testimony that he will share with you in Chapter 15. Simon Peter's brother is now a professional soccer player in Uganda, so they both overcame great difficulties to be where they are today.

Simon Peter wasn't in the audience when I was performing in 2006, but I met him later in 2009. When we started the Hope Fellowship, he joined, in part because he knew that Sylvia was an important part of the vision. He helped grow the ministry by embracing the message and inviting many of his friends, some of whom are the leaders today.

When the Hope Fellowship began, the group followed the usual model for a fellowship meeting. That was a problem, however, because the young people needed much more than regular praise and worship if they were going to deal with the issues of abandonment. Through all those early meetings, Simon kept the group alive.

Most of the early members were actually orphans, having either one or both parents die. Soon we discovered another significant culprit behind the emotional wound and that was the African custom of polygamy where children and wives competed for scarce resources. Children were often forced out of their homes by one of their stepmothers. Sometimes they tried to kill the children from another wife and, of course, the children never felt accepted into the family. Then when they married, the stepmother was still a driving force and the young couple didn't know what to do with her to minimize her influence.

Olive's sister is a beautiful young woman, two or three years older than Olive, and is married with two or three children. I recently asked Olive how her sister was doing, and she responded that Harriet had recently left her husband. Harriet was always getting sick, and a woman visitor came to her and said the reason she was getting sick was because the visitor was performing witchcraft on Harriet.

The visitor warned that unless Harriet left her husband, the woman would kill Harriet using that same witchcraft. Therefore, Harriet left her husband and her two children with that woman who wanted to kill her. Now, Harriet is wandering the streets with nowhere to go, all because of witchcraft, which stemmed from jealousy, which is rooted in covetousness.

My publisher told me a story of a pastor in Kenya

whose father had five wives. He would live with each of the wives one night every week, and then, and only then, could the children of that wife approach or talk to him. If he talked to his father on any other day, he got a beating. Can you imagine the pain and confusion from that? Yet the Hope Fellowship was becoming a source of healing for these students, and they were able to spread that healing to the University, their siblings, their families (including some of their wicked stepmothers), and their villages.

Once these children are healed from the Orphaned Heart, they are living and creating new customs that include monogamy and family values. They are committed not to repeat the sins of the past that caused the problems in their lives. They understand where they have come from and what God has done for them, and they are the standard bearers for a new generation that has said, "Enough is enough. It stops with us."

The first conference we had in July 2011 concerning the orphan issue was important because it was the time I realized the role spiritual healing needed to play in correcting the orphan dilemma. I didn't know that's what it was called yet. I did know, however, that there was a wound in the orphan's heart, and I simply labeled it the "orphan heart." I first used that name when I was standing in my driveway before I left for this conference with my friends, Cheran Cherok and Dr. Wendy LeMarquand. The wind was blowing and, as I looked up at the trees swaying, I heard the Lord say that this would be the most important thing I would ever do in my ministry. That was humbling and made me shiver.

Dr. Wendy had more experience with inner healing prayer than I did at that point, although I had been in several training sessions and was ready to get started. Cheran is an excellent organizer and intercessor, and to this day has been a powerful prayer warrior in my ministry. I was glad those ladies were coming with me to make presentations and to mentor us all in the process. They both did a great job and were a tremendous blessing to the Africans in attendance.

We worked with Hope Fellowship when we arrived, and invited clergy from various East African countries with whom we had a relationship to come and hear about this concept. There were also some people from the staff at Uganda Christian University who came. One Anglican priest named Bisoke Balakenga, who worked with more than 800 orphans, came from the Democratic Republic of Congo. He was invited by an American minister who was staying in the same Ugandan hotel where I was. The American had overheard me discussing the conference topic at breakfast. and was intrigued to hear about the event and theme. He asked if he could invite Bisoke who he thought would benefit greatly from the experience. Bisoke came, two people from Sudan arrived, and Qampicha from Kenya came along with several other clergymen, representing seven countries at that first event.

As I mentioned in the Foreword, Bisoke spoke up during the conference and said Africans knew they suffered from something, but never had a name for it. He learned in our time together that it was the "Orphan Heart," which was the root cause of so many spiritual problems like civil war, polygamy, abandonment, and poverty. Bisoke and others were able to trace some of the most common problems in Africa back to the orphan wound that created the orphan heart. The people at the conference embraced the concept in an astounding and enthusiastic way.

I did some of the teaching and counseling, but Dr. Wendy did most of the inner healing teaching. She was a wonderful guide through all the spiritual components that comprise healing prayer. Since it was the first time we were doing something like this, we all sensed something had been birthed. During our days together, the question arose about why we were using the name "Orphan Heart," since the Africans promoted the event as a conference for the Broken Heart. They had changed the name on our conference promotional banner because they felt no one would come if they saw advertising for the "Orphan Heart Conference." Therefore, they had used the name Broken Hearted.

Interestingly, the people present were the ones who made the decision not to use Broken Heart from that time on. As the conference concluded, I asked what they thought we should name the problem. By that time, all of us experienced the truth of all the concepts at the conference, saw the theological thread of the orphan heart in the Bible, and understood the theological basis for the wounds of anyone who had suffered from its effects. It was unanimous that the orphan heart was the problem, and that was what we would call it.

I explained earlier that the word for orphan is the same word as "discard" or "to throw away garbage." That was another reason we had shied away from the word *orphan*. After we discussed it, I suggested positioning the word so that it was not an identity but a condition, thus the adjustment to *Orphaned Heart*. This form of the word indicates that something was done to them as they were afflicted with the injustices of society, family, or government, especially as children. "Orphaned" indicates it is a wound that was done to them, and makes it something they could be healed from – hence the name Healing of the Orphaned Heart was permanently adopted.

Since then, I've never received any pushback when I use the word *orphaned*. The Hope Fellowship continued to be an important part of my work there in Uganda, and I went back six months later in January. The focus of this conference was impacted by the advice of Bishop John Guernsey from Virginia. He recommended I give many of the teaching opportunities to the Africans and critique them. His reasoning was that the sooner they can teach, the faster the spread of this healing would happen.

Also, my vision was that the weekly meetings of the Hope Fellowship would provide a place of support and healing for those victimized by the Orphaned Heart. That would only come with open discussion and processing the wound through sharing one's story. I needed to get back to continue to guide what the Hope Fellowship would look like – it was critical to the ongoing healing of members.

It's tragic how often people don't know their story in Africa. Even the African-American community is afflicted with this problem, since many of their ancestors came to the U.S. because of slavery, causing their heritage to be lost. In the United States, however, people are a bit freer to tell their story if they are from a divorced family or have some other broken past. In Africa, however, people are much more hesitant to disclose something personal since their culture attaches so much shame to people's personal problems. Therefore, we started in 2011 to strengthen and equip the Hope Fellowship on campus for more effective healing ministry.

The Healing Delegation

Bishop John Guernsey, a mentor of mine from the beginning and a wonderful man of God in the Anglican church, traveled to the University to spend time with the Fellowship leaders in order to mentor them. As a result of our second conference in January 2012, based on his advice and mentoring, I changed the focus of the ministry. He told me that everything I did from that point on needed to be strategic if I wanted it to really become a movement of the Holy Spirit. The most important thing, in his mind, was to build leaders who could teach so that I could multiply my efforts and have Africans speaking to Africans.

With this strategic change to help spread the healing message through trained leaders who had attended conferences, I began what I came to call the Healing Delegation. These are made up of Hope Fellowship members who have attended a few conferences and have then taught some of the subject matter. Some members of the Healing Delegation develop expertise in certain subjects like the diagnosis of the Orphaned Heart, or what it means to be a child of God. Some delegation members become skilled at handling registration, conference logistics, or worship. They minister together beautifully and it is a sight to behold. The goal is to send them out as part of a Healing Delegation to spread the message to their villages and communities.

In July 2012, I returned to continue training the students from the Hope Fellowship as they carried the bulk of the teaching. We also solidified our relationships with some of the University staff, especially the counseling department under the leadership of Joseph Masalo. Joseph is a forward-thinking man in terms of counseling, which is also not a common practice in Africa. There is a counseling center at the University, which is pretty much unheard of throughout the rest of East Africa. Joseph was our first patron and sponsor on campus for the Hope Fellowship.

The counseling department was a good way to start, but it really didn't fit with the future of the Hope Fellowship, because the Fellowship emphasized more of a spiritual rather than counseling approach. Counseling helps individuals discover why and how they became wounded, but the permanent spiritual healing can only happen through the power of God. Eventually, the Fellowship came under the oversight of the University chaplaincy department, where it remains today. We have a solid relationship with the counseling department, as I see the need for those two to have a strong connection to each another. Sometimes the problem is psychological and counseling helps significantly, and people's inner healing can happen even more effectively when healing prayer is used concurrently.

Traveling to Sololo, Kenya on My Own

I made the most of my trip to Africa and returned by myself to Sololo, Kenya in July 2012 to see Tumaini Academy's progress and participate in other important events. That's when I saw the water tank and P-2 and P-3 being built at the Academy. I also witnessed the establishment of the Marsabit Diocese, in which Sololo is located, by the Anglican Church, with Rob Martin from the U.K. as the first official bishop of the new diocese. It was under the inspired and strategic leadership of Bishop Rob, with Sue his dedicated wife by his side, that this important diocese was made permanent. Marsabit had only been a missionary diocese since it was so remote and spread out. They set their guest list, which was about 1,000 people, including many dignitaries including the Most Reverend Eliud Wabulxala, the Archbishop of Kenya. They estimated that they needed two bulls to feed everyone, and I heard the women singing while they cooked the bull through the night, realizing then that it was quite a ritual for this significant celebration. Going alone to Kenya gave me a new type of courage for adventure.

Why East Africa?

For my graduation project from Trinity, I did an independent study titled, "Healing the Orphaned Heart in East Africa." I identified and described five points as to why God would start that movement in East Africa. I saw many reasons why it would start there and eventually make its way to the United States from Africa, instead of the other way around. We think Africans need help from us, but believe me, I have learned so much from them, and I am a better person and more effective missioner because of these relationships.

One of my five points was that they are community oriented, much more than we are in the West. They understand the importance of and need for extended family to bring about real healing, because people have to have a sense of belonging somewhere if their biological family can't provide it.

Another reason is that the Africans are usually much more spiritual than most Westerners. The African traditional religion, even though it is not Christianity, has elements that make it a good primer for Christianity. One element is that it is monotheistic. Even though they have many gods, they acknowledge one creator god who fashioned all of the heavens and the earth. Most Africans believe the spirit world is more real than the world they see around them. That's what makes it a great place to teach about and promote spiritual inner healing.

It's shocking how much of their past the Africans don't know, or if they know, don't admit because there is so much shame attached to the stigma of being an orphan. This is part of the challenge we face when we try to get someone to take in a kinship child. If they do take a child in, they often won't tell others who that child is or why they have taken them in. The child won't admit to why they are there. They almost always pretend that they are with their biological parents. Consequently, the children end up living a lie.

Sylvia told me the story of a village where the kids were taken in by families. When the foster parents die, the biological children get fabric tied around their waist as a sign of mourning, but the adopted children don't. That may be the first time that those without fabric find out they are not biological children. Often after that, they are evicted from the house.

Jesus said in John 8:38 that the truth will set us free, and I am a firm believer in the truth found in that verse when it comes to inner healing. When children are told the truth, at the right time and in the right way, it may be painful, but it sets them free. That was why I began this Orphaned Heart movement and Hope Fellowship — people must have a place to share and understand their story. God can then heal the roots of rejection and abandonment, once the truth is brought to light. By the way, this applies to Orphaned Hearts anywhere in the world, not just in Africa. Anyone who has suffered from the pain of rejection and abandonment can have the Orphaned Heart even if they are not a physical orphan.

Before my month-long mission trip to East Africa 2014, the Lord gave me a sense that I was on a "big mission." That is exactly how my trip can be described. We held two conferences in Uganda sponsored through an Anglican diocese, and we conducted all conferences in partnership with these dioceses and not only under our own banner. It is easier that way to market the events to the membership in those groups.

Establishing Hope Fellowships

When we considered the needs of the organization sponsoring the conference, we realized that a vital part of ongoing healing was to establish other Hope Fellowships made up of the attendees at the conference. Our first missions coordinator, Paul Agaba, was quite adept at establishing and following up these Fellowships. He would find and equip one of the attendees as the president who could coordinate and plan weekly meetings.

Also, we always identified a patron to be the covering and spiritual oversight of the Fellowship. Usually it was the Anglican priest or the school director who invited us to come because they already had buy-in to the concept. These Fellowships are important to us and we continue to periodically train the presidents and sometimes the vice presidents. We follow the model the Holy Spirit ignited at Uganda Christian University and this proves to be the heartbeat of this Holy Spirit movement. These fellowships continue teaching and nurturing the healing process, instead of reaching random people from all over at conferences who return home and never meet again after the event.

Inner Healing Prayer – A Short Summary

In 2014, we also started doing more inner healing ministry. Inner healing prayer has been the spiritual key for individual transformation from the Orphaned Heart to the heart of a child of God (sometimes called Sonship). We focus on taking time to model and minister this gift from the Holy Spirit during all conferences, trainings, meetings, and clinics, so that people can see it in operation. It was clear from the start, however, that this concept was foreign to those present. They are spiritual people, but to pray about healing the past was a new idea. They enthusiastically received this healing, yet sometimes felt uncertain about how to lead an inner-healing session.

The Africans honor their ancestors, but they won't acknowledge or talk about their own story, let alone pray about it, as I have pointed out. It was obvious that they had to be free from that limitation if they were to be healed. When I prayed for someone to receive inner healing, I usually had someone come up who was comfortable being a model. I prayed over them and it was usually for the healing of some painful memory. Once the attendees observed or received the miracle of inner healing and realized that Jesus was present to heal them, they were open and not hesitant. I also showed them that there is biblical support for the actions we were taking. They cherished receiving the healing, but were hesitant to pray for others themselves, which is why we continue to do so much training.

Over the years since our first conference in July of 2011, conferences have become the most effective and lasting tool to bring the biblical and psychological truth to the people of East Africa about the Orphaned Heart. The conferences are welcomed by the people and the Church, and we have many requests from bishops and other clergy in East Africa to bring our three-day conference to them. The Holy Spirit message of this healing is spreading, and we are delighted! Our main limitation is the funding needed to bring our teams to people hungry for our message.

Conferences are expensive and we keep searching for creative ways to bring the message to the people at much less cost. For example, the Healing Delegation (the trained leaders in Uganda and Rwanda) has found that teaching through clinics once a week for three consecutive weeks is also very effective, and we do not have the added expense of accommodations with three meals a day for an average of 80 attendees. When God limits the resources, human ingenuity can step in and find creative ways. We still find the three-day conference to be most effective, and we are always prayerfully looking for financial partners to sponsor more conferences.

Making Adjustments to Offer Specific Trainings that Are Age Appropriate

From my experience with attendees of all ages,

there are advantages of offering this healing to a particular age group. The best time to begin to address some of the wounds of our childhood is when the Holy Spirit begins to make us aware of our brokenness. The Holy Spirit knows when we are ready to deal directly with these things, but it seems that the conferences are most effective for those who are attending college, ages 18 to 22. I believe that is why God brought me first to college students at Uganda Christian University. Of course, the Spirit is not limited to any age group, but this age bracket is particularly open for several reasons.

At this point in life, the Holy Spirit is often bringing up memories and feelings which have been put aside or covered up because of the pain and trauma from the past. College-age students are beginning to see their lives more objectively after they are away from their families. They begin to be aware that they need to be healed and are open to ideas to help them on the healing path. Those who attend a Healing the Orphaned Heart Conference at this stage of life can begin to break down the psychological defenses they created to protect themselves when they were children. Ironically, it is these very walls of protection which must eventually be brought down to heal from the past so they can change the course of their future and be freed from the Orphaned Heart.

After a conference, we encourage all attendees to form or join a Hope Fellowship to continue to embrace the healing God has for them along with those who are in similar situations. It is possible for a college-aged student to come through four years with other students on the same healing path and develop a new spiritual family searching for and finding God the Father in their lives together. By the time they graduate, they can be freed from many of the symptoms of the Orphaned Heart and can then make healthy life-defining decisions about important things such as who they will marry, how will they parent, and what is their life calling and career path.

Inner Healing and Younger Children

I am often asked, "When can children begin to face the wounds inflicted (often unintentionally) upon them by adults in their lives?" In order for children to survive, God puts a defensive covering over their hearts so that they can survive and mature. The Holy Spirit has showed me the best method to help children heal is actually to prevent the layers of calluses that can continue to be laid over their hearts from pain and trauma. Children need to know they have a great God who can come to their aid in any situation. All they need to do is to look for Him or call to Him.

When our team goes into an orphanage, we give the children a different perspective of God's presence. We begin to talk about the fact that Jesus is with them all of the time — He never leaves their side. As I found in my childhood, imagination is a gift from God that He uses to show that He is with us. In fact, it is with a sanctified imagination that faith is activated because we cannot see God with our physical eyes, but rather we "see" and sense Him with our spiritual eyes. With sanctified imagination, we know and feel that God is with us.

At this point, we can ask the children to talk to Jesus directly about what is concerning them or making them sad, and invite them to ask Him to be their personal Savior. We also ask them to receive the Holy Spirit so that

God is inside of them, able to comfort them at any time. We also find it a powerful experience for them to ask God to be their Heavenly Father. In this way, they can begin early on to understand that they are children of God and can go right to the Father with any need or concern. In this three-fold mediation and prayer, the children invite each of the persons of the Trinity, Father, Son and Holy Spirit, into their hearts and souls in order to receive the fullness of God in a way the children can embrace.

I saw a vivid example of these truths in the summer of 2015 when three children, ages seven, eight, and nine, came to a healing conference in the Diocese of Bunyoro-Kitara in Uganda. They were sitting together in the front pew, and I was concerned about what they would understand at their age, or if anything would upset them. I especially was unsure as to whether these little children were too young to benefit from inner-healing prayer. At one point during the conference, we were addressing the healing from losses in our lives. I asked the attendees to write down one loss, to allow Jesus to grieve that loss with them, and then to ask Him to fill up the loss with His very self. Then I asked the attendees to break into groups of three or four to pray for each other. I immediately walked up to the three little children and asked if I could be the prayer guide for their group. Each of them did not hesitate to show me what loss they had written.

1. Liberty, aged seven, wrote that when she was four, a friend told her that her mother had died, but that friend had lied. Her mother had not died. Liberty was traumatized and spent the whole day grieving the death of her mother, until she found out the truth. Through inner healing prayer and seeing the

80

scene in her spirit, I asked her to close her eyes to see Jesus. She did so and saw Him at the scene when she was four by her side. I then sealed her healing using anointing oil, making the sign of the Cross on her forehead and saying, "May Jesus always show you the truth, remembering that you can trust Him"

2. The little boy, Ivan aged eight, said he had lost his faith in God. I asked him to close his eyes and tell me what he saw and if he could picture Jesus. He said, "I cannot see where I am going. My eyes are covered, but I can feel Jesus taking me by the hand and leading me." I sealed his healing by saying, "Anytime you do not know where you are going, let Jesus take your hand and lead you to safety."

3. The other little girl, Frannie, was crying because one of her parents had died. I asked her to see if she could see Jesus and with her eyes closed, tears started running down her cheeks. She said to me, "I can see Jesus. He is wiping my tears away." I sealed her healing by taking my index finger and wiping away her tears, saying, "Anytime you are sad, you can go to Jesus and He will wipe away all of your tears."

That was not the end of my experience with these little children. The next day at the Conference, they were in the same pew together when we were praying for the healing of memories. I again asked if I could be their prayer guide. Liberty told me they were fine and that she was going to be the prayer guide. I asked if she needed any help and she declined. That was how confident they were in the healing power of the Holy Spirit. I came away saying to myself, "Inner healing prayer can definitely be used with little children." I am no longer hesitant to offer inner-healing prayer to children because I know the experience Liberty, Ivan, and Frannie had with Jesus will stay with them the rest of their lives. All of these spiritual tools laid a foundation for them to know that Jesus is real and is with them, secure in His love.

Later, I will describe more of the components of healing prayer, but in this next Section, I want to outline some of the problems in society that have led to the Orphaned Heart epidemic. We will look at covetousness, polygamy, and pride since those sins have caused so many problems. Then we will examine healing prayer along with the symptoms present when anyone is afflicted with the spirit of an orphan. Finally, we will look at how you can pray for yourself or for others as you confront the symptoms of the Orphaned Heart in those closest to you.

SECTION THREE

•

THE PROCESS OF HEALING THE ORPHANED HEART

Chapter 8

Rwanda Partnership

My first experience speaking to an Anglican priest about the concept of healing the Orphaned Heart was in August 2010 at the All-African Bishops Conference in Entebee, Uganda. My dear friend from the U.S., Alison Barfoot, who works as the assistant to the archbishop of Uganda for international relations, recommended I just go and hang out at the conference to meet a few clergy who may be instrumental in spreading the Orphaned Heart message.

While "hanging out," someone introduced me to Reverend Louis Pasteur Kabayiza from the Diocese of Nyanza in Southern Rwanda who was there with his wife Rose. We spent three hours talking about the conditions in Rwanda and also about the Orphaned Heart healing concept. Louis came away from that meeting saying that it was exactly what his people in Rwanda needed to heal from the horrors of the genocide. He became instantly impassioned.

It encouraged me because at this point the message was just an idea. Louis has been a rock-solid partner with our ministry ever since. In 2016, he was honored by being named an archdeacon in his diocese.

In January 2012, the Archbishop of Rwanda sent several people to the Orphaned Heart conference, including Louis. Two others were Eric Mwizerwa and another was Emmanuel Mujuni, who later became the first East African coordinator for Orphaned Heart Ministries. Both men went back to Rwanda and told the archbishop that Rwanda needed to host its own conference to help people heal from the infamous 1994 genocide that took the lives of almost one million Rwandans in just 90 days. In July of 2012, six months later, we held a conference in Rwanda.

I didn't know Eric very well, and he told me when I first met him that he wanted to get married. Realizing I would be coming to Rwanda for the conference, Eric asked me to be his mother in his wedding ceremony because his mother had died in the genocide, and he had never had a loving mother after that. Because I was teaching about the Orphaned Heart, he wanted to have a mom, who understood that concept and how it had affected him, to stand with him during his ceremony. I sensed God's prompting to accept, so some of the ministry team stayed behind an extra week after the conference, living with three other Hope Fellowship leaders. These were some of the first members of the Healing Delegation, and they now do the training and organize the conferences for Orphaned Heart Ministries. Some others in the delegation also stayed for the wedding.

The conference in Rwanda was a wonderful experience. The people came with humility and openness, and that always creates the perfect atmosphere for God to move. I discovered there are still members of both tribes in Rwanda who don't talk about the effects the genocide had on their lives, which as I described earlier is common among Africans.

The conference was held in the capital city of Kigali, and was a healing time for many. A bishop was present who was assigned by Archbishop Rwaje to be the spiritual overseer at the conference. Rev. Francis Karemera, a warm and loving leader, was also there from the diocese as the organizer and conference coordinator. The program speakers addressed the spiritual nature of the genocide and the spiritual implications of the aftermath. We helped them understand the Orphaned Heart and how the atrocities affected the souls of individuals. Even if they only witnessed it, they were still traumatized.

We also did something for the first time at this event and it involved Bishop Emmanuel. I asked him if he would perform a ritual that I called *standing in the gap* that I had learned from my mentor, Bishop Guernsey. We asked Emmanuel, as a bishop and leader, to stand in for the Church and represent it before God and the people during one of our sessions.

We did this because in some ways the Church had been complicit during the genocide. It seemed impossible for people to be healed in the Church if they could not once again trust the Church, the only place anyone should be able to receive true healing. Bishop Emmanuel stood and proclaimed to the people, "As a bishop in this Church, I ask your forgiveness on behalf of the Church that some of the hierarchy of the Church were involved in the genocide. Please forgive us as I stand here representing them."

He said that, but then he went beyond what I had asked him to do. He requested that the people and leaders from other countries come up and join him. I represented America, someone else came up to stand for Uganda, and so on. He then directed us to stand in the gap for people and repent for our countries regarding how each one responded to the genocide. In fact, the world responded by doing nothing and allowing the genocide to occur, so everyone took responsibility for their country to ask forgiveness of those present.

I was standing in the front of the room and they placed a young wonderful man in front of me who was in charge of youth in the diocese. I didn't know exactly what I was going to say as an American, but I heard myself tell him, "I am so sorry for how America sometimes uses its influence as a superpower, and I don't know how that impacted all of this, but forgive us for not responding well to situations like what happened here in Rwanda. Forgive us for not responding to the genocide and not coming in to try and do what we could, even though we knew about it."

He stood across from me and looked into my eyes as if he was examining my soul for what seemed like a long time. Then the tears welled up in my eyes as he was looking in my eyes, and he said, "I believe you and I forgive you." It's interesting that he had to believe me first, so he searched me to see if I was being truthful. Perhaps he had encountered other people who said they would help or do something, only to make themselves look good or feel better at that moment, with no intention of following through.

After we had completed that part of the service, Bishop Emmanuel prayed to break the spirit of the orphan in Rwanda, coming against various spirits and breaking curses. I could not do that as an American because there is a hierarchy of spiritual authority that principalities and powers understand. I had no spiritual authority in Rwanda but the Bishop did, and that is why it was important for him to stand in the gap.

I prayed and asked the Lord to show me the sin that had allowed this atrocity to happen, that had contributed so deeply to the orphan problem. I was never judgmental of what happened in Rwanda, for as part of a fallen, sinful race, I realized that anyone is capable of doing what had happened. My own country has its own sins of the past where other races are concerned, so God gave me an attitude of humility during the entire standing-in-the-gap process.

I had prayed that the Holy Spirit would show me what the root sin of the genocide was, because I was stunned at what happened in 1994 in this beautiful country with such wonderful people. Sin can happen anywhere. It has no geographic boundary. Things didn't become clear to me until I stood as the mother in Eric's wedding. Prior to the wedding, during our stay in Eric's home, Eric told me he had never had someone who could act as a mother in his home. I wasn't familiar with what would be required of me as a mother at a Rwandan wedding, and no one took the time to inform me either. I stayed in his home and stood with him in faith.

The first step for the wedding was when I met Eric's lovely bride named Esperance. To prepare me for my role, they took me to the town square in Kigali where we shopped for a mother-of-the-groom dress. Needless to say, that caused quite a stir. People were looking at me, wondering who was this white American woman getting a Rwandan mother of the groom dress. We found a dress and it was traditional and colorful, and I looked quite the part.

My next duty was to meet Eric's stepmother, with whom he did not have a particularly good relationship. She was part of the wedding and they had dressed us in the same outfit. That was not a mistake or socially unacceptable because I found out later they wanted us to match. While we were preparing for the wedding that week in Eric's home, it was like vacationing with my children, Simon Peter, Janet, Dennis, and Eric. I actually took them to the beach on a lake and we had a lot of fun while also bonding as an extended family. For some reason, I needed it and they needed it, too.

Eric wanted to tell us his story, which I had never heard. One day during the week, Eric talked to us in his home for about three hours, and I have never heard the likes of such a testimony. Many testimonies have emerged from the Rwanda genocide, and this one is just as intense and moving, if not more so.

As a side note, from this point on I am going to honor the wishes of the Rwandan government that is trying not to focus on the names of the tribes who were involved. Rather than identifying with one particular tribe and feeding the division, the government hopes the people would identify with each other as Rwandan citizens in order to create unity. Therefore, I will call the one tribe the "aggressors," and the other tribe the "victims," as I relay Eric's story.

On the first day of the genocide, Eric and his family escaped by taking refuge in his church. On that day, he had seen his grandfather and other members of his family killed. This particular church, which was his family church, had served as a safe haven two years prior when there had been trouble, so they thought they would be safe. All the churches had been safe places, but in 1994, the aggressors did not hesitate to enter the sanctuaries. On that fateful day when he saw his grandfather and other members of his family killed, a memory that still lingers with him. Eric later found out that approximately 32,000 people were killed that day on the grounds of his church. He said there were also helicopters hovering above the church using machine guns to kill, besides killers with machetes on the ground.

From the first day and for the next 100 days, if you were from the victim tribe, you were hunted down like an animal. Eric, who was 14 years old, lived through the first killing at the church by hiding under bodies for about four hours. Then the aggressors came back, wearing different outfits. They pretended to be from the tribe of the victims and told them that it was safe because the killers were gone. They asked anyone who was wounded to come out. The wounded did come out, as did Eric. Then the aggressors revealed their true identity and had the victims stand in two lines. One line was for people with money and the other for people without.

The people without money were killed with a machete. Eric was terrified but had the sense to stand next to a woman in the line of people with money, even though he had no money. They went down the line, made each person hand over their money, and then shot them. The woman next to Eric was holding a baby. When she surrendered her money, they shot her and the baby. She fell on Eric, so he was once again saved by being under a dead body, this time staying under her for eight hours. He was one of four people who lived out of the 32,000 killed in that area that day.

The aggressors called the victims of the tribe "cockroaches" on radio broadcasts that played over loud speakers for all to hear, and kept broadcasting murderous threats all day, stirring the aggressors to slaughter. I assumed there were days of killing and days of inactivity, but that was not the case. Eric said it was non-stop killing. Eric saw his mother, who was a strong Christian, killed in the next day or so. He reported that she was wearing a white dress. Of course the killers and the victims all knew each other. One of Eric's friends was from the aggressor tribe. When he saw Eric, he told him to come with him because they had his mother and Eric could die with her. At that point, Eric related that he wanted to die, losing all desire to live. One would think he would have run, but he didn't. He went with his friend because there was no place to go.

When he arrived with his friend, Eric saw his mom in a clearing where the women from the other tribe were goading the aggressor men to kill her, for the women collaborated with the men in carrying out the genocide. Eric's mom had a Bible and was reading the verse where Jesus said to forgive them for they know not what they do. She was praying, and her tormentors were yelling at her to stop praying, but she refused. Then the angry women directed the men to strip her naked because they wanted her dress. Eric told us there were about 20 women present. Practically speaking, that many women were not able to share one single dress.

After thinking about it, God revealed to me that one of the major reasons for the genocide that brought so much pain and suffering was the sin of covetousness. Coveting is the last sin of the Ten Commandments, and is a more potent motivator than envy or racism: "You shall not covet your neighbor's house. You shall not covet your neighbor's wife, or his male or female servant, his ox or donkey, or anything that belongs to your neighbor" (Exodus 20:17). The aggressors coveted something, so the angry women kept pressing to have her killed. They did eventually take the dress and her life, and Eric saw all that at the age of 14. Then he somehow escaped, hiding underneath the roots of trees and in swampland and any place he could hide his body from sight for 90 days, while he struggled not to die from starvation.

The sin of covetousness is a sin that knows no end, for it never satisfies those it motivates. Those who covet and take something don't truly own anything, for eventually it will pass away, just like the money they took from the people before they killed them. That money was going to evaporate and disappear, and only leave the covetous desire for more money. It may sound strange, but the aggressors actually coveted the beauty and the very lives of those they killed. When covetousness goes viral, the end is death.

Covetousness is insatiable. You will find the sin of covetousness is the root cause of any genocide you can name or research. It was present in Nazi Germany when the Germans confiscated all that the Jews owned, and eventually took their lives. The Germans coveted what they had and, in order to get it, they committed genocide. The Russians coveted what they saw in Eastern Europe and Ukraine, so they began to practice genocide. When you covet, nothing you do will satiate your desire. It can end with you taking another person's life, even when the covetousness innocently started with envy or jealousy.

I returned to Uganda after the wedding and preached at a Hope Fellowship meeting about what I had seen. While I was doing my preparation for my message, I further realized that Eve coveted the one thing she couldn't have, which was what God had, and that was the knowledge of good and evil. Satan tempted her by asking her why she shouldn't have it too, and tempted her to covet what only God could have. Later in Genesis, Cain coveted Abel's acceptable sacrifice and so he killed his brother Abel. It was the first account of murder in the Bible. In both cases, the root cause was covetousness.

One final word on this before we move on. People have to dehumanize others to enable them to plunder and murder. That's why they call each other demeaning names, such as cockroach. It was the same in the U.S. with racism and slavery. During the Jim Crow era, people of color were depicted as stupid or sexual predators, and therefore anyone who harassed or killed them was doing society a service.

If the aggressors can dehumanize their victims, then they feel justified in taking what belongs to the other person, including their lives. Yet, it's a cycle that cannot be satisfied by taking. Even when a life is taken, there is no satisfaction, and it becomes a compulsion to keep trying to take more. Proverbs describes covetousness this way: "The leech has two daughters. 'Give! Give!' they cry. There are three things that are never satisfied, four that never say, 'Enough!'" (Proverbs 30:15). It can't get enough blood or suck enough life out of anybody to be happy or satisfied.

I am not saying that covetousness is the only symptom or cause of the Orphaned Heart, but I learned in

Rwanda that it can overpower the mind of the aggressor tribe; they are tricked by the enemy to feel justified in committing violence against the victim tribe. In studying the history of what happened in Rwanda, anger was building, and resentment between the two tribes was fueled by the preferential treatment of European countries that were ruling over the people. In the next chapter, I will identify some other root symptoms of the Orphaned Heart before I close this Section with a basic outline of the teaching we offer at our Orphaned Heart conferences.

Chapter 9

The Stronghold of Polygamy

Polygamy is embedded in the culture and minds of the East African people, for it has been practiced for generations. It is prevalent and a widespread practice, although many Africans have begun to speak out against it for various reasons. In the last chapter, I mentioned it as a social ill. It may sound strange or counterintuitive, but polygamy is actually a major contributor to the Orphaned Heart problem. You may ask, "How can that be? I thought orphans did not have any parents? A child of a polygamous relationship would still have a mother and a father. Isn't that better than having no parents?"

You are correct that those children do usually have two parents, but the ramifications of multiple children from multiple wives create social dynamics with almost the same conditions as if the child were without parents. In fact, in some cases it is worse. Let me give you some biblical examples of what happens when there are children present with one father but multiple wives.

The first story to look at is Joseph in the Old Testament. Jacob, Joseph's father, had two wives who were sisters — Rachel and Leah. The first dynamic that we see in their story is the competition between the two women for the affection of their husband Jacob. How did they compete? They tried to have more children than the other woman.

Leah had no problem having children, but Rachel struggled. It was customary then for the wife to have her maid serve as a surrogate mother if the wife could not conceive, so Rachel had Jacob sleep with her maid Bilhah and she conceived two sons. When Leah saw that Rachel's maid had produced a child, she urged Jacob to sleep with her [Leah's] maid, Zilpah, and she also produced two sons, in addition to the six sons that Leah had produced. Thus, there were three women producing children for one man, ten in total.

Eventually, Rachel was able to conceive and she gave birth to two sons, Joseph and Benjamin, but Rachel died at childbirth when Benjamin was born. That made four child bearers in one family with one father. Since Jacob loved Rachel more than Leah, he favored Rachel's two sons above all his other sons. When you read the biblical account of this polygamous family, you see that it produced disastrous results. Here are some of the ramifications that Jacob and his wives produced:

- The ten sons hated Joseph and Benjamin.
- When Rachel died, Reuben, son of Leah, forcibly raped Rachel's maid, Bilhah, to dishonor his father and make an arrogant statement against Rachel's

offspring.

- Jacob's sons to Leah, Simeon and Levi, sought revenge for their only sister Dinah being raped, and tricked her rapists into a false sense of security before they murdered them all.

- Jacob gave Joseph a many-colored coat, which stirred rage and jealousy in the other ten.

- The ten were violent, conspiring to murder Joseph, ultimately content to sell him into Egyptian slavery.

- Once Joseph was sold, they lied to their father Jacob that Joseph had been killed by a wild animal, and perpetrated that lie for the next 22 years! They said it so long they believed it themselves, which is why they could not recognize Joseph when they later were in his presence in Egypt.

- Judah, one of Leah's sons, visited a prostitute and impregnated her, only later to find out she was his widowed daughter-in-law, whom Judah had refused to provide for after his son's death.

Each one of the sons exhibited traits consistent with an Orphaned Heart. The competition for love, the violence when it was not found, the deception and hatred — all of those characteristics come from a wounded heart that has suffered rejection. They had a mother and a father, but they still had an Orphaned Heart.

The second story to consider is that of King David. There are some who believe that David was the illegitimate son of Jesse, although Scripture does not support this directly. What does seem odd to so many is that when the prophet Samuel came to anoint one of Jesse's sons as king, Jesse had to be reminded that David even existed!

When David was anointed as the next king, his brothers hated him. Eliab scolded David when David came with relief supplies as the army of Israel battled the Philistine army. Eventually, not one of David's brothers or family members became part of David's military guard or royal government.

David was a brilliant warrior, musician and song writer, honing the latter two skills during many lonely nights while he was shepherding his father's sheep. David was a man after God's own heart, but David had one problem — he was unable to curb his sexual impulses, which is another trait of those suffering from an Orphaned Heart. David took multiple wives, and each one produced offspring. As in Joseph's story, the children did not mix well, and David seems to have been an aloof father who was not present to discipline his sons. What was the result?

- David, the man after God's own heart, conspired to murder so he could take one more wife named Bathsheba.
- Eventually, one of David's sons named Absalom conspired against his father to seize the throne and would have killed his father if he had the chance.
- Prior to that, Absalom took revenge on a man who had taken sexual advantage of his sister named Tamar. Absalom took revenge by taking the man's life.
- Even on his death bed, David neglected to make plans for his succession, refusing to intervene in the family squabbling and jostling for position that had already begun to take place.

Let's fast forward to the twenty-first century and

see if there are any similarities between what we see today and what we read in the stories of Jacob and David. Here are just a few of the common problems faced in modern nations as the Orphaned Heart condition explodes:

- Overpopulation due to wives trying to outdo each other by having more children than their rival wives – they believe they have more power with their husband.
- Wars between tribes and nations.
- Misbehavior among warring troops that includes rape, theft, confiscation and betrayal.
- Competition among wives in polygamous marriages for affection, limited food and male attention, and marriage partners for their own children.
- Revenge being sought for perceived and actual wrongs done to clans.
- Rampant sexual sin.
- Poverty due to children having to share what little they have among the parents, children, and all their step brothers and sisters.

These children of polygamy become parents eventually. Without some specific intervention, they carry that Orphaned Heart with them – it will not become whole just by outgrowing it. Therefore, they will repeat the same patterns that they experienced as children. Until they are healed, they parent from the Orphaned Heart, meaning they are distant, looking at their children as a means to become more powerful, rather than as a means to give life to the child for love's sake.

As parents they become self-focused rather than focused on the welfare of the children. I had a driver once in Uganda who was the youngest of 29 children. Obviously, his father was a polygamist and was a poor man in his village. He kept having children, however, because that was his way of becoming what my driver referred to as the "big man." Even though he bragged about the number of children he had, he never did a thing for his children.

As we saw in Jacob's example, the wives in a polygamous relationship become competitive, sometimes to the extent that they will try to kill the children of the other wives. They will perform witchcraft over those other children, trying to harm and destroy them, even if they are so-called Christians. It is tragic that often the husband stands by and does nothing, even though he knows his wives are feuding. Maybe it's the fact that the women are fighting over him that contributes to his sense that he is a big man.

The children of polygamy also become leaders in their communities and in clans. If leaders aren't healed from the Orphaned Heart, all the traits of the Orphaned Heart manifest in their relationships and roles the leader has to play. They can abuse their power because of their Orphaned Heart. In East and West Africa, we have seen multiple military coups. One leader will take over from another leader, and then each one will be just as notorious as the previous one. If you study their lives, they have all come from orphaned or polygamous situations. Their childhood was filled with difficulty because they didn't have a loving mother and father, and they became pawns in the jealous rivalry between mothers.

Explanation of Chart Contrasting Hearts

God created us in His image, and that image was

meant to be instilled and reinforced in a family. If you refer to the chart that contrasts the Orphaned Heart with the heart of Sonship (page 122), you will see that one of the Orphaned Heart traits is the need for approval. If leaders have a heart of Sonship, they don't strive for the acceptance of man. When leaders function from an Orphaned Heart, they need approval. They strive for praise and acceptance of others. That is why they surround themselves with people who will tell them what they want to hear. They will lavish gifts and promotions on those people, or turn on them when those people do not deliver.

People suffering with an Orphaned Heart live by the letter of the law, and can be dictatorial, even as pastors. They see everything as black and white. It's difficult for them to forgive anyone who wrongs them — family, followers, church members, or friends. They wield power and it feeds the hole in their Orphaned Heart temporarily, but it's a bottomless pit and cannot be filled or satisfied.

Leaders with an Orphaned Heart enter into intense competition and rivalry with everyone. I explained how I learned this in Rwanda with the issue of 20 women wanting one dress before a woman was killed. An orphan doesn't know where his or her next meal is coming from, so they grab what they can today. When that fear is reinforced, it exhibits as a "live for now" attitude. They take what they can right now and take as much of it as possible, for there may not be anything there in the future. They eliminate rivals since they are competitors for limited resources like food and love. Stealing is a common trait of the Orphaned Heart, for they don't trust that they will have what they need unless they steal.

Orphans may have to live on the streets, relying

on their "street smarts," and they never stop living that way, even as adults. They fight for what they can get now because they don't believe there is any inheritance waiting them in the afterlife, and they don't trust God that their future, or that of their people, is secure. As children of God, their Sonship secures their inheritance and they know there is eternity waiting.

I do not want to leave you with the impression that the Orphaned Heart is a problem only in Africa. It shows up in our Western cultures in different ways, but it is becoming more and more common. Our skyrocketing divorce rate is one indication the Orphaned Heart is preventing men and women from entering into and keeping the covenant of marriage. Orphans don't believe they have the capability or even the right to happiness in any relationship. Their loneliness is a perpetual curse that, unless broken, will cause them to go from one relationship to another, never finding peace or satisfaction.

The rash of single mothers is creating the same problem. Of course, there are situations that are beyond the woman's control, but when those situations occur, she must make every effort for the rest of the males in her family to enter the picture to help give her children a father's love. Yet we are facing issues that no generation has faced before, things like artificial insemination, same-sex marriage, and live-in couples. The children of these relationships will tend to have an Orphaned Heart, for they do not have the model God gave us of one wife and one husband when He created man in the Garden, and the effects of that will be felt for generations to come. As an aside, the materialism that grips my nation is increasingly the result of people looking for fulfillment in things that they never received in relationships. The problem is that their latest technological toys cannot take the place of a father's and a mother's love.

Orphaned Heart Ministries attempts to address these issues by using the sword of the Spirit to break these wrongful soul ties to past generations. We help people come to understand that they are children of God with all the benefits we have discussed so far. Back to Africa, it's difficult for fathers to show love to their children. Culturally, they aren't taught to hold and hug, and that's something so needed by their children. I have had young African men tell me their father has never really talked to them. They have a culture of being a proud man. If they are seen talking to a child, they are considered weak. We try to help the men understand that they must replace their African culture with the culture of God's kingdom, which is love, peace and joy. Simple acts like speaking and showing love can be liberating for a child and for the parents.

Returning to the Old Testament examples of Jacob and David, the good news is that God intervened and turned their dysfunction around. David was able to rise above his problems, reign successfully, and turn the throne over to Solomon. And Joseph, the offspring of a dysfunctional, polygamous home, was able to rise above it all and become the world's most powerful figure. Joseph did not stoop to the depths of his family's cruelty, but cared for his family without giving in to revenge or the traits of an Orphaned Heart. There is hope for healing the Orphaned Heart, but only in Christ. That is where the truth will set anyone and everyone free, and that is our source of strength and hope in Orphaned Heart Ministries.

Leaders and pastors in Africa are recognizing the problem and the need for healing. From the time I stepped on the ground in Uganda and delivered the message God has given me, they received it because they knew it to be true. They said they knew they suffered from something, but never knew what it was. Satan is the father of the Orphaned Heart. He is the author of all the conditions that lead to the Orphaned Heart, and wants to separate all mankind from the love of God. All his works are evil. We have to realize how important a father and a mother are to a child and do everything we can to cultivate healthy, monogamous relationships throughout life. I know it's not always possible, but that should be a goal, and to do so under the covenant of marriage.

Chapter 10

Inner Healing Prayer

Let me take a moment to explain what inner healing prayer is. It is simply prayer that focuses on healing at a person's soul or emotional level. Humans are made up of spirit, soul, and body. The soul level is comprised of the mind, heart, emotions, and memories. When we receive physical healing, our bodies are healed. Healing prayer can bring wholeness and release at the soul level. We pray for people to be healed from memories and things that have happened to them, usually in their childhood. The earliest things that happened to us set the stage for how we respond to life and how we interpret what happens from that time forward. The earlier that memory can heal, the better the chance the person has to live in wholeness.

Hope Fellowship wasn't ministering healing prayer at their meetings because of their hesitancy to pray for people to receive that healing. That's why we decided to have a day at each conference that is devoted to teaching people how to facilitate inner healing. My team was made up of 25 people, and were joined by 25 others from another ministry named Bethesda, which also utilizes healing prayer. We came together and trained those present in the techniques of inner healing prayer, using Rita Bennett's material that I had received in Seattle.

Bethesda Healing Ministries is headquartered where Orphaned Heart Ministries is in Mukono, Uganda, where Uganda Christian University is located. Their emphasis has been on deliverance. They are led by a fantastic clergyman named Reverend Captain Titus Baraka. They have about 50 members, many of whom are students at UCU. They go out as a team every Saturday to places where people need deliverance. Orphaned Heart Ministries has partnered with them and often goes out to join them and learn from them about deliverance. In 2014, my team and I led an inner-healing prayer training for them and shared how to pray for healing over their own brokenness.

They had always been praying for others, but their own wounds were still within them. Once they experienced healing from these deep wounds, especially from early childhood, they were astounded. Three young women came up to me after the conference and proclaimed they finally understood how to pray for themselves and how the Holy Spirit can heal them from what has afflicted them since their childhood. They were freed from their chains of sadness and brokenness. They now join us in our Hope Fellowship meetings, and we rejoice that we have learned about deep spiritual truths from each other!

Rita Bennett and her husband Dennis were pioneers in bringing the charismatic renewal to the national Episcopal Church. Dennis passed away in 1991, but Rita has continued the legacy of teaching people around the world about the power of the Holy Spirit to bring healing to people's emotions and heart wounds. Rita has written four books and has hosted numerous training conferences around the world. I mentioned earlier that I attended one of her conferences that paved the way for my work in Africa.

We specifically used 15 of the prayers that she had written for people to use when we trained others. We even did some work with replacement of names if anyone had been given, or called, a horrible name. For example, one man helped a young woman whose name was No Love. What would it do to you if every time you heard someone call your name, that person said, "No Love"? Rita also had developed prayers to help people correct their concept of their Heavenly Father that had been marred by a cruel or absent earthly father. Our experience with our biological father impacts how we feel about the Heavenly Father.

In 2014, I visited three different countries: Rwanda, Uganda, and Kenya. Our time in Uganda was especially significant, because the Healing Delegation went to two strategic dioceses. One was Gulu in the Diocese of Northern Uganda, where Joseph Kony commanded the Lord's Resistance Army. I desired to go there because I heard so much about the disaster that occurred among the people from his rampages. God was calling us there because there was a lot of healing that needed to take place.

Bishop Johnson received us and we had 85 or 90 people, most of them his clergy, and he was there for many of the sessions. The Bishop had a wonderful Canon in charge of missions, Canon Francis Odora. Our ministry was well received, and they thanked God that it was exactly what they needed at the right time. We imparted to them a new way of thinking about how to heal. For the first time, they realized that healing was possible, even though something so horrific had taken place. They were so wonderfully open to what we taught, and I have great testimonies from that time of how people responded.

When I went there, I found two spiritual strongholds at work that were contrary to one another. One was the stronghold of rebellion, which was the basis for Joseph Kony's aggressive rebellion. The other was the stronghold of passivity, which infected tens of thousands of people who were in camps for 18 years and never learned anything new. There is a saying in Africa that states, "They didn't learn to dig," which means they didn't take the time to learn farming or any of the skill sets to survive in Uganda. When they didn't learn how to dig, they could starve – and many did.

We also had an effective conference in Hoima with orphans from the Jeremiah Orphan Program, the conference sponsored by Christ Church of Grove Farm in Pittsburgh. Christ Church had educated and cared for the children, and the Church had planned to phase the program out after 10 years. The Jeremiah Program released the 150 children, because they had graduated, but a lot of them had no family and no place to go. After the young adults were released, the leaders realized that they still had a lot of rejection present in their lives, which was causing many problems. No matter what they did, these children kept encountering rejection. Education by itself wasn't enough for them to gain their freedom.

They had been taken away from their parents or were truly orphans. Sometimes their parents died, and at other times their parents or the extended family could not support them. That gave those children a sense of rejection that they were homeless – no one wanted them. Then they were brought into the Jeremiah Program and put into homes. After the program, they were supposed to resettle into clans, but it was difficult for that to happen for reasons I described earlier in this book. No matter how much the leaders tried to help the graduates succeed, there was always another rejection to set the graduates back. The problem was that if the spirit of rejection is not cast out and healed, the children will continue to set themselves up for rejection through bad relationships that have no chance of success.

The people at Christ Church felt that our conference would be perfect to help heal the Orphaned Hearts of the Jeremiah Program children, and that's the reason we went to have one there in the summer of 2014. We conducted a search to bring those graduates together because the program had ended in 2012. We didn't find them all, but there was a great representation along with other people present who had not been part of Jeremiah.

With each conference, we found God was helping us to see the societal root of why these children became orphans. At times, it was parents dying from AIDS. In Gulu, it was Joseph Kony's rebellion and all of the political ramifications of child soldiers. In Rwanda, it was the genocide between the aggressors and the victims. Each region had a systemic cause that fed and led to the Orphaned Heart problem.

We prayed to break some of the societal curses into which these children were born. It's what the Bible calls a stronghold, which is now an important part of each conference. Through the tree branches and roots, we see that the root cause for many strongholds are injustices. It is no one's fault. The children may have been born at a time of war when there was death, fear and violence. It is not their fault, but how they responded to it can be their sin. We address the historic environmental or sociological issues, not in a formal but a spiritual sense, factoring in what impacted the area to create the conditions for which healing is needed.

Let's spend the rest of this book looking at the ten steps that anyone can take to recognize and be free from an Orphaned Heart. These steps are the foundation for what we teach in our conferences, and I want to give you a glimpse so you will have a better idea of our approach and what we are looking for when we pray and teach. Perhaps you will find an opportunity to apply these steps in your life or in your ministry to those around you.

Chapter 11

The First
of Ten Steps

Up to this point, I have described my journey that helped me discover and develop the teaching and ministry to heal the Orphaned Heart. The journey has been part experiential, based on what I have seen and learned from my many trips to Africa. The other part has come from my studies, both at Trinity Seminary and from the many books I have read and seminars I attended on the subject of healing prayer and inner healing strategies. Of course, all of this has been steeped in both personal prayer and study of God's word to ensure that I was not veering off course or missing the mark. At this point, I would like to share with you the ten steps involved to help identify and heal the Orphaned Heart.

Some of these steps are borrowed from other practitioners who have recognized concepts and developed effective remedies. I have taught about all these steps, and I have seen them work in the lives of those who use them and those upon whom they are used. I will give credit where credit is due when I include something that someone else has pioneered and shared.

The Orphaned Heart is not just a problem in Africa, but a human problem that is not the sole possession of any one race, country or ethnic group. I discovered and developed my approach to the problem in Africa, but the analysis and cure are relevant in every culture and among all people. What's more, the basic remedy, which is steeped in prayer and the Word, is not that difficult to apply, although there are certainly deeper levels that require more experienced counselors and sometimes even professional help that goes beyond what I have described. As you read, I ask that you prayerfully consider three things.

First, be open to the Spirit working in your own life. As you read, you may sense that some of the steps would be applicable to your life to help heal some area of your own brokenness. Don't resist what the Holy Spirit wants to do, and don't be afraid. God is not out to get you, He is out to heal and set you free. What's more, you are in good hands if the Holy Spirit is the one who is leading you.

Second, be thinking of people who could benefit from this message. If someone comes to mind as you read, pray for them. Ask the Holy Spirit if you should give them a copy of this book. Third, be open to helping sponsor a healing prayer seminar near you, perhaps through your church, ministry, or community. There are many people in your midst who are suffering the effects of abandonment and rejection. You may recognize that more clearly now that you are reading this book. A prayer conference is a great way to introduce the principles. It also gives people a firsthand look at some who will be set free during the conference. Then some volunteers and staff at your church can be trained to carry on the work after the event is over. Having set the stage, so to speak, let's begin our look at the ten steps.

STEP ONE

Have a clear understanding of the definitions and concepts, based on biblical principles, of orphans, adoption, fatherhood of God and being a son or daughter of God.

When you read the early chapters of Genesis, you find the story of how the Orphaned Heart first began. In Genesis 1 through 3, we learn that when man was first created, he had an intimate relationship with God the Father in the Garden of Eden. Adam and Eve walked with God, spoke with Him, and were sustained by His word and presence. Through their own interaction with the serpent in the Garden, they sinned. That sin created a separation between them and God, which led to their being expelled from the Garden.

After that, mankind had a different relationship with God than God intended. That relationship is chronicled throughout the Bible, especially in the Old Testament. It started with the first murder in Genesis 4 when Cain killed Abel, both of whom were the sons of Adam and Eve. Cain was jealous of Abel and his sacrificial offering that was more acceptable to God than was Cain's. In anger Cain killed Abel, perhaps hoping that then God would accept Cain's sacrifice.

From that point in Genesis 4, things worsened.

God reached out, first through Abraham, to establish His covenant to restore mankind out of His great love, by creating the nation of Israel to whom He entrusted His Law. Yet mankind rejected God again and again. That struggle continued until Jesus came to Israel to establish a new covenant — the forgiveness of sins through His shed blood. Of course, we are still under the curse of the Fall, but through Christ, we have the potential to once again have intimacy with God the Father through the Holy Spirit.

When Jesus said in John 14:18 that He will no longer leave us as orphans but will come to us (the key verse upon which we built this ministry), He was basically restoring things through His death and resurrection as they were meant to be originally in the Garden. When anyone accepts Jesus as Savior, even though a sinful being, they are able to enter again into a relationship with God the Father. That means those people can have intimacy with God, even more intimacy than in the Garden, because the Holy Spirit indwells them. That means we actually have God's presence within us. We become children of God with God as our Father, but only when we put our faith in Christ to save and cleanse us.

Humans are either sons of wrath (Ephesians 2:3) or sons of God. There is no middle ground. This is exemplified in the Old Testament through two characters: Ishmael and Isaac. Isaac and Ishmael are good examples of someone who is a child of God (Isaac) and someone who is outside the family of God (Ishmael). Isaac received the blessing from his father Abraham as the son of promise, while Ishmael did receive a blessing from God to become a great nation (Genesis 21:18). Whereas the blessing of Isaac was for all generations to come and all the nations of the Earth (see Genesis 22:17-18). It is interesting that today there is still turmoil and enmity between the sons of Ishmael (Arabs) and the descendants of Isaac (Jews). There is no way to understand this hatred except through the biblical account of those two sons. Ishmael kept searching for his father Abraham's blessing, but could never find it.

This has significance for the world today. The teaching of Islam stems from the heart of an orphan. You can see the Orphaned Heart of Ishmael being created by the circumstances of his birth and the rejection by his human father, Abraham, playing out in the biblical accounts. Prophecies said that Ishmael would be a wild donkey of a man, that his hand would be against everyone, and everyone's hand will be against him. Ishmael went on to settle in lands in defiance of all his relatives.

The traits of the Orphaned Heart are the same as displayed in Islam because they emanate from the view of the father as a harsh master and not a loving father. The founder of Islam, Mohammad, was also an orphan, raised by an uncle. If true, the more the world suffers from the Orphaned Heart, both from Africa and the West, the more people will turn to Islam because they are unable to understand the loving Father of Christianity. Allah has no children. You never hear anyone call Allah their Father. Allah is remote and somehow cannot be reached. They are never sure if they touch his heart because he never talks. He is just out there somewhere, and they try to find him through prayers and other rituals.

It is clear that the Orphaned Heart is becoming a worldwide epidemic. That's why there is a propensity in many nations, even in the United States, to turn to Islam, because if someone has an Orphaned Heart, they can't comprehend God as a loving father. They will seek God, but there is an emptiness in their lives because they cannot find Him. With all of the divorce in the U.S. along with single motherhood, the concept of a loving father is fading from memory. That's why there are so many angry people trying to inflict pain on others.

The only way to really please Allah according to some is to have a jihadists philosophy, which is a violent taking of what others have, including their lives. The only way you can truly know you have inherited eternal life is through jihad. If you are a regular person in the Islamic faith, you cannot be certain that you have a right standing with God. Therefore, if you have an Orphaned Heart, you will tend to respond more to Islam.

I believe this gives us true insight about how to reach the Muslim world. They do not have an Abba (Father) God. That desire to have one, however, was birthed in us by God Himself when He wove us in the womb (see Jeremiah 1:5). We need to examine one more word or concept in Step One and that is the concept of Sonship, and I am using it as a term that denotes both genders, male and female. Sonship is restored when we become children of God through Jesus who is the Son of God. We connect with His Sonship so that when we accept Jesus as our Savior, we can have an intimate relationship with God the Father. Then the Holy Spirit comes and lives in us.

The Father offers His love to each of us, a love that came at great cost because of Jesus' sacrifice on the cross. When someone has an Orphaned Heart, that heart battles against the heart of Sonship. They are diametrically opposed to one another. If you have an Orphaned Heart, you tend to respond as an orphan, and you will have the tendencies and traits of an orphan. One of the characteristics of the Orphaned Heart is not to know about or expect any inheritance. When you are a child with no inheritance, you respond in the present and take what you can get out of life right now. Since it isn't going to be given to or provided for you, you have to take what you can by manipulation or force.

Paul talks a lot about what it is like to be adopted into the family of God. He also uses a lot of language that contrasts the child with a servant. He points out that either you are a servant or a child of God. If you have the servant mentality, you don't have all the rights of a child because you are just a servant. When you accept Jesus, you know the heavenly Father is your Father and all the riches of eternity and even blessings of this life on Earth are yours as a child of God because He loves you so much and lavishes blessings on you.

You have no fear of the future when you are a child of God, no matter what happens. You still have your human frailties, yet you have a sense of safety, a sense of home, a sense of belonging. One of the traits of the Orphaned Heart is not knowing that you have a safe place in the loving heart of a father. When that is missing, you are spiritually homeless, restless, going from one fad, one relationship, one craving to another. Genesis 4 tells us that Cain did not have a home, and so he wandered along with his descendants. They tried to create a home, but to no avail.

There you have some of the concepts and language about being a child of God, relating to the Fatherhood of God, and how we are adopted into the family of God through Jesus' work on the Cross. That adoption makes us children of God. It's such a beautiful thing to think of how Jesus prays for and loves those who belong to God the Father because they are all family — brothers and sisters under the love of one Father. When we are children of God the Father, that means that Jesus is our Brother. We truly are part of a wonderful family where there is no room for the attitude or behavior of a spiritual orphan. I will not spend this much time on each of the ten steps, so let's move on to Chapter Twelve, where I will devote the entire chapter to Step Two.

Chapter 12

Step Two

Conduct a diagnosis to understand the areas of the soul
that are affected and the depth of the problem.

To help with the diagnosis in Step Two, I refer
you to the book *My Father, My Son* by Bruce Brodowski.
Bruce developed the wonderful chart on pages 122 and
123 outlining the characteristics of the spirit of adoption
and the spirit of Sonship. Let me say it is possible for
someone to come to Christ but still be operating out of
an Orphaned Heart to some degree. When you study this
chart, it will be easier to diagnose the depths of your own
Orphaned-Heart tendencies. There may be a few or you
may have many, or you may have a little of some or a lot
of a few. That is what I mean by conducting a diagnosis.
We are not at the remedy stage yet, just the analysis. Take
a few moments to read the list.

The Spirit of an Orphan

The Spirit of Sonship

The Spirit of an Orphan		The Spirit of Sonship
See God as Master	**Image of God**	See God as loving Father
Independent/ Self-Reliant	**Dependency**	Interdependent/ Acknowledges Needs
Live by the Love of Law	**Theology**	Live by the Law of Love
Insecure/Lack Peace	**Security**	Rest and Peace
Strive for the praise, approval, and acceptance of man	**Need for Approval**	Totally accepted in God's love and justified by grace
A need for personal achievement as you seek to impress God and others, or no motivation to serve at all	**Motive for Service**	Service that is motivated by a deep gratitude for being unconditionally loved and accepted by God
Duty and earning God's favor or no motivation at all	**Motive Behind Christian Disciplines**	Pleasure and delight
"Must" be holy to have God's favor, thus increasing a sense of shame and guilt	**Motive for Purity**	"Want to" be holy; do not want anything to hinder intimate relationship with God
Self-rejection from comparing yourself to others	**Self-Image**	Positive and affirmed because you know you have such value to God
Seek comfort in counterfeit affections; addictions, compulsions, escapism, busyness, hyper-religious activity	**Source of Comfort**	Seek times of quietness and solitude to rest in the Father's presence and love
Competiton, rivalry, and jealousy towards others' success and position	**Peer Relationships**	Humility and unity as you value others and are able to rejoice in their blessings and success
Accusation and exposure in order to make yourself look good by making others look bad	**Handling Others' Faults**	Love covers as you seek to restore others in a spirit of love and gentleness

The Spirit of an Orphan

The Spirit of Sonship

The Spirit of an Orphan		The Spirit of Sonship
See authority as a source of pain; distrustful toward them and lack a heart attitude of submission	**View of Authority**	Respectful, honoring; you see them as ministers of God for good in your life
Difficulty receiving admonition; you must be right so you easily get your feelings hurt and close your spirit to discipline	**View of Admonition**	See the receiving of admonition as a blessing and need in your life so that your faults and weaknesses are exposed and put to death
Guarded and conditional; based upon others' performance as you seek to get your own needs met	**Expression of Love**	Open, patient, and affectionate as you lay your life and agendas down in order to meet the needs of others
Conditional & Distant	**Sense of God's Presence**	Close & Intimate
Bondage	**Condition**	Liberty
Feel like a Servant/Slave	**Position**	Feel like a Son/Daughter
Spiritual ambition; the earnest desire for some spiritual achievement and distinction and the willingness to strive for it; a desire to be seen and counted among the mature	**Vision**	To daily experience the Father's unconditional love and acceptance and then be sent as a representative of His love to family and others
Fight for what you can get!	**Future**	Sonship releases your inheritance!

used by permission from *My Father, My Son* by Bruce Brodowski

Did you see any of yourself and your tendencies in the Orphaned Heart column? If you did, relax, for we all suffer from the Orphaned Heart wound because we are children of Adam and Eve and because we have all been wounded by other humans, sometimes even by our own parents who loved us or abandoned us, intentionally or unintentionally. Once you have that wound, it is reinforced in life by ongoing rejection, which we all encounter, and abandonment issues that may be our perceptions more than reality. Once you have an Orphaned Heart, you see life through that condition, and it's associated with a lack of love from a parent or parents. It may just be that your father is or was not present. That can reinforce the wound, so that it cannot heal over time.

The important thing to realize about the Orphaned Heart is that you can be a strong Christian, a person who goes through therapy and a lot of other things, only to find that the Orphaned Heart wound is still there. It will be there until you go through a specific process to heal that wound. For example, if you had a severe laceration on your arm, and you didn't have it treated, it would fester and the infection could spread to the rest of your body. It's the same thing with the Orphaned Heart wound.

If you have a scar from someone who wounded you deeply, that wound has to be healed. It does not automatically heal over time, but must receive intentional attention that leads to healing. You can learn to live with the pain, but it doesn't go away. It can actually get worse if it is reopened by other experiences you have. The wounded heart is often associated with a lack of a loving father. Before you accuse me of being sexist, I need to say one thing about the lack of a mother's love.

The mother's love is called *storge* love in Greek, meaning "natural affection"[1]. That Greek word is used to represent a mother's love that is like the nurturing love of Mother Nature, which provides the things that are needed to sustain life, like water, food, etc. It undergirds, provides a foundation, and is always present. This *storge* love is foundational in a baby's development through the second year of life. Without this loving presence of a mother through affectionate touch, eye contact, and a loving tone of voice, the soul level of the child's development is stunted. They cannot say it — but they have a deep emotional wound, possibly through their lifetime, unless God intervenes in their lives. They desire emotional and physical intimacy even in their adult life. When babies receive *storge* love, the foundation is set for them to have a healthy desire for emotional and physical intimacy throughout their lifetime. While the mother's love is nurturing, the father's love tends to give a child his or her identity. We are usually called by our father's last name and belong to his clan, if your culture recognizes clans. When the mother's love is gone, there is emotional emptiness for sure. When the father's love is missing, however, there is a painful uncertainty as to who we are and where we belong.

Please don't misunderstand. There can be situations where a mother has deeply hurt someone, and that certainly creates a wound that needs to be healed. In healing prayer for an Orphaned Heart, however, we are usually looking for problems in the father-child relationship. Regardless of whether it was caused by father or mother, an orphaned spirit is a demonic spirit from Satan, and it's

---

[1] Bruce Brodowski, *A Memoir: Healing Childhood Emotional Wounds* (Charlotte, NC: Carolinas Ecumenical Healing, 2015), page 158.

a result of the Fall. In some sense, we are all born with an orphaned spirit that we inherit from our parents, who got it from theirs, all the way back to Adam and Eve.

The orphaned spirit attaches itself to our soul – our emotions, thoughts and feelings – and is reinforced by Orphaned-Heart wounds. That's the wound that comes from a person hurting us who should have loved us. There's a difference between the Orphaned-Heart wound and the orphaned spirit. When we find the orphaned spirit in a person, there are other spirits that attach to the Orphaned Heart wound like the spirit of rejection and abandonment. In fact, that's how I began this whole pursuit of healing prayer – by seeing the spirit of rejection and abandonment in people when I was in Africa.

The symptom of the orphaned spirit, listed on the chart by Bruce Brodowski, is independence. People with orphaned spirits act as if they don't need people. They may not want to let other people into their lives, and are incapable of trusting people. They don't allow themselves to be vulnerable to people or to God. They are often hostile, and have a deep anger and resentment concerning how their life should have gone. Their hostility is expressed toward others and even towards God, not knowing that a deep relationship with the Father can happen through Christ. They're contentious, often starting arguments, and they enjoy goading people to get a negative reaction.

I already referred to the story of Cain and Abel. Cain had no sense of home, of belonging, or of being a son. You can also see the same was true for Ishmael. He had no sense of home, after he was evicted by Abraham, his father. Muslims don't teach that, of course. But in the inspired Bible, we see that Abraham put his son, Ishmael, and his mother, Hagar, out in the desert where God rescued them (see Genesis 21).

When you function out of an orphaned spirit, you think like a household servant and not as a child of the house. You don't think you have a right to anything, and settle for crumbs off the table. You don't believe you have the right to the full banquet of the Father, just what's left over. That's how a servant would act and think. The orphaned spirit strives for what it can get, just like orphans who are on the streets, having to rely on their own wiles and smarts. They don't know about the inheritance waiting for them or living in eternity as a child of God, so they only live in the present and for the moment.

Orphaned spirits can often resort to competing, stealing, or begging because they have such a deep sense of competition and envy. I have already addressed the issue of covetousness. They compete and strive to get whatever they can get from whoever they can get it. A person with an orphaned spirit is afraid of intimacy, especially if they did not have *storge* love from a mother as a baby. Adam and Eve had intimacy with God in the Garden, but that was broken and what was produced was the orphaned spirit. The orphaned spirit manifests through addictive behaviors, as it desperately looks for ways to heal the wounds that only God can heal. Those are some of the ways that the orphaned spirit acts out in life and relationships.

A spirit of Sonship acts in the exact opposite manner. The Father offers his extravagant love to each of His children, and they respond as God's children as eternal members of God's kingdom who have a full inheritance for which they do not strive or work. The father's love pulls the child up to live to his or her full potential, while the mother's love, that *storge* love, undergirds them. The Father pulls them up to a future inheritance and their purpose. That's what the father's love can and should do.

You can conduct your own diagnosis with the questionnaire and the chart provided. Take a moment now to review the chart again, and then answer the nine questions on the following "Impact of Abandonment and Rejection Questionnaire":

1. Reviewing the chart, which orphan heart symptoms do you share, if any?
2. Have you experienced rejection or abandonment? If so, how and when?
3. What God-given needs have not been met as a result of being abandoned and rejected?
4. How have others responded to you in this situation? For example, have you had some people who have helped you?
5. How have you coped? What have you done to satisfy any unfulfilled needs?
6. What habits or self-destructive behaviors have you developed to meet those legitimate needs?
7. How did you feel about your parents? Your care-givers? Your culture? Is there a sense of rejection/abandonment/shame?
8. How can these legitimate needs be met?
9. What words are you waiting to hear from a parent which were never spoken to you?

By completing this, you will be able see if you have any of the symptoms just discussed or on the chart. Have you known rejection and abandonment? Out of that rejection and abandonment, are you aware of needs that have not been met because you have been rejected and abandoned, usually by a parent? It's more common for fathers to abandon the home as we see happening in Africa and the U.S.

When that happens, children are aware that there is something wrong, something lacking. The important thing in determining how deeply you are affected by this is to look at how you respond to certain situations. If someone tries to help you, how do you respond to that? Those with the Orphaned Heart are defensive. They have a hard time accepting help or trusting people because they have never been able to trust their father. How could they now trust someone who promises something and risk never having it fulfilled?

The more you are aware of the Orphaned Heart wound and the more you embrace your need for healing from it, the faster your addictions will lessen. You won't have that hole in your heart that you try to fill with sex, shopping, multiple relationships, drugs or video games. Obviously, I believe in therapy and endorse any and all recovery programs like AA or other 12-step programs. But the hole will always be there until there is healing of the Orphaned Heart and freedom from the orphaned spirit.

Until you are healed and free, you will continue to respond sinfully to your needs. You will think, "I deserve better. I'm the most important person." You are actually coveting what someone else has or what you think you should have. You don't really understand what you should have, because you're not in a place to make rational decisions. You're operating from your subconscious and not from your conscious. You are not secure as a child, but insecure as an orphan.

We all suffer from the Orphaned Heart. It's only the degree to which we suffer. Once you complete the questionnaire, study Brodowski's chart, and if you say yes to even a few of them, you have symptoms of the Orphaned Heart. Because of the Fall and how it affected all of us, everyone can benefit from this healing. The Cross came to reverse the effects of the Fall, but it isn't automatic. You cannot accept Jesus and expect everything to be okay. You have to confront these issues with intentionality. It's like taking an island in a war. Jesus made a beachhead in your life, but now together you have to take the whole island. There are pockets of resistance everywhere, some that you easily see and some that are more hidden and underground.

This is why we refer to sanctification – the process of becoming holy – as a walk and not just an event. Some people have likened healing prayer and deliverance to peeling an onion. You peel off one layer and then there's another one below it. You pray and get victory, but then you are facing something else. You may wonder where that new thing came from. It came up because you went a little deeper, saw a little more, became more mature, were capable of facing the next steps. You may wonder what you did wrong because you thought the issue was gone. Don't be surprised when you confront something in your heart and then go back and have to deal with it again. It doesn't mean it was incomplete. It just means you are better equipped to handle the truth.

There is a danger in terms of going back into your past, and that is wishing that you could go back, romanticizing the way you were. Let's say as an example that someone is an alcoholic and they romanticize the fun they used to have when they were out partying and drinking. When that happens, they will return to that lifestyle because they enjoyed the pain, drama or sense of temporary control it gave them.

Jesus said, "No one who puts a hand to the plow and looks back is fit for service in the kingdom of God" (Luke 9:52). Don't glamorize your past, and don't abandon the hard work it will take to get healed. Don't allow yourself to go back, even though it calls to you regularly. In life, it's sometimes two steps forward and one step back. Go back, but only to get your healing. Then move on.

In the next chapter, we will cover Steps Three through Five. Let's go there now.

Chapter 13

Steps Three
Through Five

STEP THREE

Begin to share your story with good listeners who
God will provide, preferably in one-on-one or small
group sessions with those on the same healing quest
of understanding.

My awareness of the Orphaned Heart began when
I was performing. I don't know how many people stayed
after that failed concert, perhaps 300, to discuss being an
orphan or orphan problems. That was in 2006. Many of
those people stood up to share testimonies and stories,
even though it took a while to get them to start talking.
When they started talking, it was like someone opened the
floodgates. Many shared what it was like being an orphan,
including the shame of being one or the shame of caring
for orphans. They talked about anything connected to the

word *orphan* because the word means garbage in their language. There was a lot of freedom and crying through those vulnerable moments when people shared. I asked the pastor who had arranged all of this how many times his people had talked about the orphan problem. He said by his recollection it was the first public discussion about the orphan situation. No one ever talked about it, but there was a measure of healing that day because people shared, talked, and listened.

Part of the reticence to talk in Africa is because it will reflect badly on the tribe or clan. In theory, the tribe or the immediate family is supposed to step up and step in to help the abandoned child. That's what is supposed to happen, but it often doesn't happen. No one wants the extra responsibility, and often they cannot afford to take on another mouth to feed. Therefore, the child is left on his/her own, leaving him or her vulnerable to abuse or violence. That child must take to the streets or be subject to an abusive relationship, unless they find an orphanage – or an orphanage finds them.

I discovered that when children were taken in as babies, they learned to call relatives 'mother' and 'father,' and often didn't know they were orphans. Then one day, as I shared in Chapter Seven, they are shocked to learn when the supposed "parent" dies that they are indeed orphans. They then encounter unspeakable shame at having believed a half-truth for so long. Another thing I discovered is that people may never say they were orphaned because they may not even know it. When they understand their own story and are able to express it, they have taken a large step toward healing. The same will be true for you.

This is why we started the Hope Fellowship after that first meeting at Uganda Christian University. We wanted a place where people could share the way they had shared in that first public meeting. The problem was that when I wasn't there, the meetings tended to become more like a church with services that included worship, a message and all the rest. We have tried to lead and equip them to take on more of a support-group atmosphere where people can share freely and others can support them.

One of the first and most important steps toward healing is finding a support group that will help you find and keep your healing. I met an Anglican priest in Gulu who was born on the side of the road. His mother lived through that birth, and so did he, but they named him "Almost as Good as Dead." That was his given name, *not* a nickname, because he was born on the side of the road.

His mother took him home and he couldn't breast-feed the first or second day, probably because they were both traumatized and malnourished. She was thrown out of the home by her mother-in-law, who told her if she couldn't breastfeed, then she must leave. The baby stayed and she left. By the time I met this little boy, he was a 55-year-old priest who had been raised by his grandmother. This priest wept openly as he told me this story of how his mother left. He didn't know why she left, but he thought she had abandoned him for almost his entire childhood because she didn't love him. He never knew that she had been kicked out of the home.

Finally, his mother came to him when he was 18 and told him that she was his mother. He was filled with anger, because he thought she had simply deserted and left him behind. No one had told him the real story. He told her she was like any other woman to him, and she left crying. Then sometime later someone told him the real story, that his mother was forced out of the house. He was so sorrowful and tried to find her, but she had died, which only served to increase his shame.

When I talked to him, he still had that wound. He was a perfect example that if someone had told him, even though he may have had anger at those who kicked her out, he would not have felt she rejected him. He was living with this pain even at the age of 55. Jesus said the truth will set you free, and He was correct. I'm a big believer in the power of sharing your story. We found a lot of people in Gulu who had received inappropriate first names because of the circumstances of their birth, just like that priest had been. Step Three is telling your story to those who will treat the story with confidentiality and respect, who will be part of the solution and not part of the problem.

STEP FOUR

Prepare the spiritual pathways for the Holy Spirit to work in you. Accept Jesus into your life, renounce evil and cult-like behaviors, and invite the Holy Spirit into your heart.

The Holy Spirit does the work in our healing, and so the question is: How do you prepare yourself to have the Holy Spirit work in you? First, you must accept Jesus Christ as your personal Savior, because you cannot have the Holy Spirit unless you have put your faith in Christ to forgive your sin. That's the first thing. Second, you renounce evil and cult-like behaviors. To help you with this, I refer you to the Freedom from Bondage Checklist designed by Rita Bennett (used by permission). It's important to read this chart because we often don't know the acts or deeds we have done that keep us from God's blessings. What's more, God cannot reside in a place where there is evil or unforgiveness. You must renounce these things with which you were inadvertently or consciously involved.

Freedom From Bondage Checklist

Check on left "R" if repented of;
on right "P" if prayer needed

Have you, your father or mother, or their ancestors been involved in any of the following?

R. P.

☐☐ Had your fortune told by the use of tarot cards, tea leaves, palm reading? Tried to foretell the future?

☐☐ Been involved in astrology? Deuteronomy 18:10

☐☐ Practiced meditation or allegiance to any god other than the God of the Bible?

☐☐ Believed in reincarnation? Matthew 16:14; John 1:21-27

☐☐ Studied or practiced clairvoyance, levitation, telepathy, automatic writing, water-witching (divining), astral projection (soul travel)?

☐☐ Been involved with "mind science" in any form: EST, "Christian Mind Sciences," "Mind Control," Scientology?

☐☐ Studied or followed occult philosophies or cults: Yoga, Transcendental Meditation, Eckankar (out of body travel), Eastern Religions, Buddhism, Zen Buddhism, Islam, Hinduism, Confucianism, Taoism, Rosicrucianism, or other cults? Deuteronomy 18:9-14

R. P.
☐☐ Denied the Trinity, the Deity of Christ, His blood atonement for sins, His bodily resurrection, or His Second Coming?

☐☐ Believed or taught that all religions will save us ("we're all going to the same place")?

☐☐ Been a subject of Trance Hypnotism (spells)? Deuteronomy 18:1

☐☐ Practiced witchcraft?

☐☐ Consulted stars or spirits?

☐☐ Attended a séance or healer meeting of any kind?

☐☐ As a medium, tried to contact the dead (necromancy, Spiritism, spiritualism, shamanism)?

☐☐ Used a pendulum, sandals, or other fortune-telling device or consulted a medium or healer?

☐☐ Carried or wore a charm you have placed your trust in rather than God?

☐☐ Possessed any occult or pagan religious objects?

☐☐ Tried to cast a magic spell, put a hex on anyone or gotten someone else to do it for you? Deuteronomy 18:10

☐☐ Made a blood pact with someone? Deuteronomy 18:10

☐☐ Read or studied in the realm of magic or the black arts?

☐☐ Viewed television programs or films which dealt with the occult (i.e., "Rosemary's Baby," "The Exorcist," "Poltergeist," "Silence of the Lambs," etc.)?

☐☐ Smoked mind-altering drugs or any other drug for mind expansion or spiritual experiences?

R. P.

☐☐ Been addicted to alcohol or other addictive substances?

SEXUAL INVOLVEMENT that is outside of God's plan for marriage as described in the Scripture leads to strong bondage that needs to be broken in the same way as occult involvement (1 Corinthians 6:9-10; Romans 1:26-27; Jude 1:7)

☐☐ Viewed pornographic pictures, films, TV shows, Internet?

☐☐ Sexual fantasy coupled with masturbation; any compulsive, immoral sexual behavior.

☐☐ Read pornographic books, magazines, and novels?

☐☐ Any unbiblical sexual behavior, i.e. homosexual sex (both genders). See list that follows.

☐☐ The following is a biblical list of heterosexual homosexual sins that break fellowship with God and make one vulnerable to demonic oppression or invasion: fornication, adultery, compulsive masturbatory sex, sodomy, heterosexual sex (both genders), bisexual sex, sadomasochistic sex, incest, pedophilia perpetrator, transvestite – transsexual sex (with self or another), prostitution, group sex, or bestiality (1 Corinthians 6:9-11; Exodus 20:14; Leviticus 18:6-30; Matthew 18:6, 10; Genesis 19:1-11; Romans 1:24-32; Jude 1:7; Deuteronomy 22:5; Proverbs 5:7-14 5:20-23; Leviticus 18:23; Deuteronomy 27:21).

I use this checklist because it is comprehensive, and gives a complete overview of typical practices that perhaps once seemed innocent, but have serious spiritual implications. For example, if someone has had a consultation with a witch doctor, as some have done in Africa, then they have to renounce that because they sought help apart from the guidance or help that only God can give. That person chose something God forbids and there are spiritual implications for that. If you have used the Ouija board, which is more common in the West, you must renounce that act.

The first step toward freedom is identifying those things on the checklist and then praying the prayer that is also included in this book entitled "Renouncing the works. Prayer steps for freedom from bondage." By doing this, you are preparing yourself spiritually, because for you to be healed from the Orphaned Heart wound is to allow the Holy Spirit to heal you. This checklist and prayer will remove those things that can hinder and block the Holy Spirit from working in you without your awareness.

Prayer Steps for Freedom From Bondage

- Confess to God as sin anything believed, studied, or practiced that is displeasing or contrary to His Word.
- Ask God's forgiveness for being involved in these things.
- Promise to no longer have anything to do with them.
- Promise to burn or in some other way permanently get rid of books or equipment connected with them at first opportunity (Acts 19:19).
- Speaking softly, specifically renounce the cult or false occult teaching in the Name of Jesus.
- Speaking softly, bind by name any spirit connected

with that belief, study, or practice under the Blood of Jesus Christ. Break the power of that spirit and command it to leave; deny it permission to return (Mark 9:25).

- Thank God for what He is doing.
- Repeat the second step for each cult or false occult teaching with which the person has been involved.
- Renounce Satan and all his works.

Once that is completed, we then proceed with a simple invitation for the Holy Spirit to come into your heart. This is not what some refer to as the baptism of the Holy Spirit. It is a specific invitation for the Spirit to come into that part of your life where the blockage had previously existed. In our conferences, we spend a minute where people actually say, "I welcome the Holy Spirit into my heart, mind and body, and I ask Him to direct me and lead me as He sees fit." The words are less important than the act and decision of inviting the Holy Spirit into you, all of you. In a sense, this fourth step is like cleaning house to make room for a new guest, who is the Spirit of God.

STEP FIVE

Ask forgiveness and repent from any sinful ways you responded to rejection and abandonment from parents, society, or cultural injustices.

I am sure there were real wrongs perpetrated against you over which you had little or no control. That is a common human experience in this Fallen world. What you did have control over was your response, and your sinful response to a sinful situation was or is still sin. If you were rejected and you tried to find love in all the wrong places with all the wrong people, then you must take a moment and ask God to forgive you. That is where the tree illustration on the next page comes in. This tree is important because it shows us that the roots of the tree are things like injustice, generational patterns, and curses, but then there is flagrant sin. Those first things, the soil or the roots of the tree, were not our fault. At this point in my seminars, a person may need to grieve over an injustice committed against them. For example, if their father died in war and their mother was left without any resources, they may have experienced extreme poverty. It is interesting that even poverty is often a result of the Orphaned Heart wound that has become systemic in a tribe's or country's culture.

If that person's father died in war, he or she must grieve over that injustice, because he or she did nothing to deserve that injustice. Sometimes I allow time for people to grieve over what might have been had it not been for the injustice. In some sense, they mourn for the lost opportunities of youth or life. The most important point, however, is for the person to consider how he or she responded to those injustices. That is the part of the equation over which they do have control.

People who lost a father through war maybe became involved in a lot of different sexual relationships to try to heal that wound and fill that heart void. This is their sin that they must acknowledge and for which they need to ask God's forgiveness. That's a powerful liberator when someone is able to ask forgiveness and see their role in their dilemma. Without that, they have a victim mentality, believing that their problems are *all* because of others.

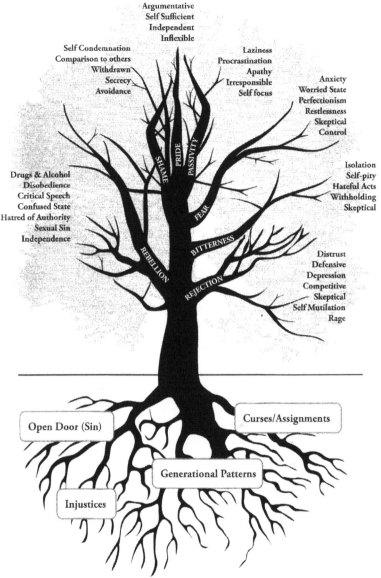

Most of their problems may be the responsibility of others, but there is always something for which they must take responsibility by asking God's forgiveness for their sins. This act gives them a power to be transformed through Jesus Christ, otherwise the victim mentality will continue.

143

That is an important takeaway as you or anyone studies that tree. In the United States, for example, we have seen society develop cultural injustices such as happened when African Americans were enslaved and treated as less than human for centuries. Of course, that is not their fault. Yet an ungodly response to an ungodly situation opens people to more problems, and they must see that ungodly fruit was nurtured to maturity on that tree through anger, resentment or revenge. They cannot deal with the roots, but they can deal with their own bitterness, anger or unforgiveness. That is the goal of Step Five.

Let's now move on to the last five steps in the Ten-Step path toward healing the Orphaned Heart.

Chapter 14

Steps Six Through Ten

STEP SIX

Forgive through the power of Jesus Christ, especially forgiving those who caused the earliest wounds of rejection and abandonment.

Forgiveness is taking responsibility for your role in the problem and going to God to ask Him to help solve it. You take responsibility for your attitudes and behaviors, whether it's unforgiveness, anger or resentment. When you acknowledge your role, God is willing and able to give as the Lord's prayer tells you: "Forgive us this day our trespasses, as we forgive those who trespass against us." When you forgive those who have caused your earliest wounds, it will set you free and is the quickest means to bring about change in your life. You might consider it an "offensive weapon" to remove the power that person or that injustice has over you. If we do not forgive them, they are still maintaining some degree of influence or control over our emotions and our reactions. Forgiving them removes their influence over our lives and enables us to move on.

Someone once said that we are like marionettes with cables attached to us that make us dance. Unforgiveness is one of those cables that makes us dance to the wrong tune with the wrong dance steps. When we forgive, it's like those cables are cut and we can move about with immediate freedom. I have heard many people say after they have forgiven someone, even perhaps someone they never even knew or met, that they felt lighter. That is the immediate power of forgiveness.

God provided the most powerful and sacrificial example of this forgiveness when Jesus forgave those who were crucifying Him right on the spot while He was dying (see Luke 23:34). Rita Bennett developed a wonderful meditation that I use in conferences where we imagine ourselves at the foot of the Cross, and allow ourselves to hear Jesus say that He forgives us because we realize now what we did. We receive His healing, and in that moment of meditation, we step away from the foot of the Cross. Then we ask the participants to see the person they need to forgive coming over the hill. Sometimes the people can't see who they are at first, but they allow the Holy Spirit to bring that person to them whom they must forgive. Often, the people have not recently thought of that person, but the Holy Spirit knows the heart and knows whom they must forgive. It might be a recent relationship or someone they never met, like a deceased parent.

Then I ask that they picture themselves and this person both at the foot of the Cross and hear Jesus say to the person who hurt them, "I forgive you, for you did not know what you did to wound [insert their name]." Then the person who was rejected or abandoned inserts his or her name at the end as if Jesus was saying this. It goes like this: Jesus says, "I forgive you, mother of Susan, for you did not know that what you did would hurt Susan." The person who was wounded can actually hear Jesus say those words and, while He is forgiving them, He isn't diminishing the fact that they were hurt by that person, but He forgives them nevertheless.

He is also not forgiving them without being specific. That is important for healing because the person hears Jesus acknowledge the thing that happened to them was wrong, but that He forgives the person who inflicted the actual pain. After the person visualizes Jesus healing the party who hurt them, how can the person who was wronged do any less than what Jesus did? Then it's time for the wounded party to do their own work of forgiveness right then and say that they forgive that person just as Christ forgave on the Cross. That is often one of the most powerful times during the conference, because the Holy Spirit is present to help set the people free from the effects of resentment and unforgiveness.

STEP SEVEN

Break the power of generational sins.

We have conference participants who have experienced the same things happening in their families over and over again, from generation to generation. These events or conditions can be suicide, depression, poverty, inability to maintain relationships, or addictions. Going back to the tree, you see one of the roots of the tree is generational patterns. These were inherited by or passed down to the children through no fault of their own. It's important to allow God to bring those things to the surface so that the participants can see what those issues are. This can be done through analysis of ongoing problems or by asking family members to identify people in their past, perhaps people they never knew, who may have been involved in demonic practices or Satanic worship.

It's important that those ties be broken over this present generation, and that can only be done through the power of the cross of Christ. We read in Exodus 20:5-6 that those sins have implications to the third and fourth generations.

> You shall not bow down to them or worship them [idols and false gods]; for I, the LORD your God, am a jealous God, punishing the children for the sin of the parents to the third and fourth generation of those who hate me, but showing love to a thousand generations of those who love me and keep my commandments.

We have people complete a family tree, naming the people back to the third or fourth generation, and identifying the things that those people might have suffered from. If you go to www.christianhealingmin.org and look for the menu item "Forms" and then click on "Family Tree," you can download a worksheet to help people identify on that tree those who might have done something that still has spiritual ramifications today.

Of course, orphans or those not raised by their families have a difficult time doing this, so we rely on the Holy Spirit to help them use what little they know to construct their tree. At times, people praying for them will help discern some of the issues they may be facing.

For those who are able, we try to go back to the third or fourth generation and then break wrongful soul ties by putting the Cross of Jesus and the Blood of Jesus between that person and a prior generation. Using the sword of God's word, we sever any and all destructive influences from the past. Once again, I borrow a tool from Rita Bennett, this time a prayer that I find has the power to break those wrongful soul ties from past generations. This prayer can cut some of those marionette-like cables that control people to respond the way they do. We then review the pardon that is promised in Ezekiel 18:19-22:

> "Yet you ask, 'Why does the son not share the guilt of his father?' Since the son has done what is just and right and has been careful to keep all my decrees, he will surely live. The one who sins is the one who will die. The child will not share the guilt of the parent, nor will the parent share the guilt of the child. The righteousness of the righteous will be credited to them, and the wickedness of the wicked will be charged against them.

> "But if a wicked person turns away from all the sins they have committed and keeps all my decrees and does what is just and right, that person will surely live; they will not die. None of the offenses they have committed will be

remembered against them. Because of the righteous things they have done, they will live."

If the curses can be carried forward to future generations, then the blessings can go forward as well, and sometimes embracing the blessings from past generations is a great thing to do as people acknowledge the positive aspects of their family's past.

STEP EIGHT

Receive inner-healing prayer in groups of three that include people who have been trained in such prayer, or who are spiritually trustworthy.

The goal of Step Eight is to see that memories are healed as prayer is administered and focused. Rita Bennett describes this as the theology behind inner healing prayer. The Trinity is a triune being, or three persons in one. We have three parts to us also in our being, which is the spirit, soul level, and body. All three levels are under the curse of Adam, but when people give their lives to Jesus and ask Him to be their Savior, they have the Holy Spirit of God in them. Their spirit is made pure and connects to the Holy Spirit, for our holy God does not mix with evil. It is through the connection of the Holy Spirit with our purified spirit that our soul and physical level can be healed by God.

As explained earlier, at the time of the Fall, man was cut off from God with terrible implications for man's emotional and intellectual life. The soul level is where the healing must take place so we can experience change in our personhood. The physical body is also sometimes healed when there is healing at the soul level. That happens often, and somewhat surprisingly, although it should not be a surprise, for medical research increasingly shows that the body is deeply impacted by one's emotions and thought life. If people, for example, have unforgiveness, they might find when they begin to forgive, their back pain or arthritis goes away. I have seen that occur after healing prayer. Of course, there are physical problems that are uniquely physical that were also caused by the Fall, and the source of those is not the Orphaned Heart. I have seen powerful physical healings too – we never put anything beyond the healing touch of God.

This inner healing prayer is important because it heals at the soul level. When we look back at the first seven steps, we can see that these steps involve our will, understanding, and mind. Those steps help us identify some of the things that need healing because of our behavior, our personal history and generational patterns. Step eight, however, is where the soul is truly healed.

Judith MacNutt states that when we receive a healing on the soul level, it's just as powerful and permanent as any kind of healing that might happen on a physical level. The soul is complex and like a multi-faceted diamond. Each time we receive an inner healing on the soul level, one of those facets is polished. What's more, it's a permanent healing. That is why I recommend praying inner-healing prayer as often as possible. I do that myself. I want more and more facets polished so that my soul shines brightly to honor God's work in my life

Think about all of the things that could have wounded us or things that have happened to us in our lives – the injustices, the generational curses, the people who hurt us, knowingly and unknowingly. We are ripe and primed for a life of brokenness. Inner healing prayer provides that special healing on the soul level.

Medical research is finding that *all* our memories are stored in our brain, even if they are not at the conscious level. These memories may even be stored from when we were in our mother's womb. I have seen God move miraculously to heal many painful memories that people did not even know were present in their minds. Yet the first step is that people must know Jesus Christ as their Savior and be able to receive the Holy Spirit to have inner healing prayer effective at this soul level. Sometimes people have to experience healing of a memory in order to have a wall broken down to even receive Jesus. Sometimes their misunderstanding of who God is has kept them from God.

I highly recommend some healing prayer precautions because we are dealing with people's spiritual lives and must be careful. For example, I recommend you have someone serve as a guide for people as they go through their inner healing. That guide should have some training and experience. There also should be an intercessor close by who is praying for the presence of Jesus to be there, and also for the Holy Spirit's leading.

It's also good to have a scribe who is writing down the prayers or what is being said, because rarely do those being prayed for remember everything that is going on. At that moment of healing, the guides are allowing themselves to be a vehicle for the Holy Spirit, and should not be distracted with taking notes. The person being prayed for should be involved in the moment and not thinking about how they are going to remember this, so the scribe is for their benefit as well. The account of what occurred is another source of healing and encouragement when it is read later on.

There are a lot of people who are skilled at inner healing prayer all around the country, especially in the U.S. It is not common in Africa, but we are trying to remedy that. I have been trained by Rita Bennett and Judith MacNutt primarily, but I have also read a lot of books from other authors. Rita Bennett has a whole list of prayers that we consider inner healing prayers because they heal at the soul level. Some of them are for healing memories, but some of them are for things like separating our image of God the Father from our human father, as I previously mentioned.

I am not opposed to using prayer forms that are standardized because I have seen them work. It's not about relying on a specific formula, but it is about helping a person come before God and be transparent and open. If a godly prayer that someone else developed can do that, I am in favor of using it.

One of the beautiful inner healing prayers is when a person utilizes the Lord's Prayer as an intercessory tool. I have also had Psalm 23 prayed over me as a prayer. As the words are spoken, the person praying lingers over the words, allowing the person receiving prayer to see themselves walking with Jesus. They walk through the valley of the shadow of death with Jesus, using the power of their imagination.

Rita actually has a prayer to cleanse the imagination as a preparatory prayer so that it can be used as a cleansing tool in the healing process. It's great to be with a group you trust who has had training, has a firm biblical foundation to be doing what they do, and who can recognize and utilize the presence of the Holy Spirit. Without those people, I would be careful about going too far in the prayer process.

STEP NINE

Find a safe spiritual family of believers to continue your healing through inner-healing prayer, Bible study, accountability, and love.

We were born to a mother and a father. We have a genealogy, a family tree and we have what is behind us and what is in front of us. A lot of our pain comes from our natural family, so they may not be a safe or healing family. When you are with them, there may be things that push your buttons and cause you to revert to old patterns and feelings. In Mark 3:33-35, Jesus asked, "Who are my mother and my brothers?" Then he looked at those seated in a circle around him and said, 'Here are my mother and my brothers! Whoever does God's will is my brother and sister and mother."

Jesus Himself had a spiritual family with the disciples with whom He traveled, and that did not include His natural family. Jesus' family did not understand or support His mission, so He had to be careful not to surrender His work to their unbelief. You need your own family of believers to continue the healing process to be free from the Orphaned Heart.

In Africa, we created our Hope Fellowships that I have described. We try to form one wherever we have had one of our conferences. I want this group to meet so people can learn to trust each other, because everyone is a believer in Christ. I want this group to be proactive when it comes to promoting one another's healing. The more proactive they are, the more they will see God move, and the faster and deeper they will heal. They will encounter an amazing walk with others with the Lord present in their midst.

I don't pretend to be a therapist. I am more of a spiritual guide and facilitator in all this, and I am eager to train others in these principles so they can be utilized and applied in churches and small groups. The students at Hope Fellowship at Uganda Christian University told me several years ago that, through applying the principles and praying for one another, they didn't have the Orphaned Heart any longer. They could actually see and feel the healing.

They noticed how they were responding differently, and their lives were changed because they weren't seeing things through the filter of the Orphaned Heart. It's remarkable to see that they are in community and accomplishing this together. There really is hope for change when we have a family of believers walking with us. The healing must be intentional and ongoing, however, or else the progress will fade and people will revert to old patterns. It's the same principle that orthodontists use when they are straightening teeth. They may straighten the teeth, but the patient needs to wear a retainer to keep the teeth straight, to maintain the progress that has been made. Without the retainer, the teeth will eventually go back to their original position. Hope Fellowships help retain the ground the Holy Spirit has won for those who are part of the Fellowship.

STEP TEN

Pass this message on to others you love where God places you to work, live or fellowship.

The greatest way to continue healing in your life from an Orphaned Heart wound is to help others heal. The more you do that with others, the more you will find your own wounds healed. That's what we do in Africa in more and more places, by creating Hope Fellowships. Then my Healing Delegations go out to spread the word and minister to other people.

All people at times seem reticent to share their story, and I have told you the struggles that Africans sometimes have in giving a testimony that includes their past. There are several passages that may provide you and others the incentive to share your healing journey.

The first is Revelation 12:11, which states, "They triumphed over him by the blood of the Lamb and by the word of their testimony; they did not love their lives so much as to shrink from death." There is power in your testimony. It helps you to triumph over your past, and also to maintain that victory. It also helps other people as they hear what God has done for you. It gives them hope that God will do it for them.

The second is what Jesus told a man whom He had delivered from many demons: "As Jesus was getting into the boat, the man who had been demon-possessed begged to go with him. Jesus did not let him, but said, 'Go home to your own people and tell them how much the Lord has done for you, and how he has had mercy on you'" (Mark 5:18-19). The man wanted to travel with Jesus, but Jesus sent him home to testify about what God had done and how he had been set free.

The third and final (although there are more) is from Matthew 10:27: "What I tell you in the dark, speak in the daylight; what is whispered in your ear, proclaim from the roofs." Jesus wants you to get into the habit of sharing what He has done for you, and what He has taught you. That is in part why I am writing this book — to share in public what I have spent hours learning in private. You must find ways to do the same, and encourage those whom you see set free to do the same.

Chapter 15

Testimonies From The Field

Throughout this book, I have mentioned numerous people with whom I have a relationship because of the Orphaned Heart message. I want to give three of those people a chance to talk about how the message has impacted their lives as we close this book to give you an idea of why I am so passionate about seeing Orphaned Heart Ministries become all that God wants it to be in East Africa and other parts of the world. Here are the three testimonies.

Olive Nyamuhunge

My name is Olive Nyamuhunge, and I am citizen of Uganda and a student in the United States. I study ministry with social concerns at Palm Beach Atlantic University. I would love to work in any organization that reaches out socially to people, especially foster children and orphans.

Living here in the United States has required a

significant adjustment, especially with the culture and the college. The studying has been very different and more challenging than back home in Uganda. By the grace of God, He helped me come here, so I am confident He will help me come through it all. He is doing a lot of great things for me, and I am excited about that.

Obviously, when I was young, I didn't have much mature thinking. You are mostly just thinking of playing and getting along with people like young children do. At the age of seven, when I met Janet and Worth, I thought they were very sweet, very nice and so kind. And they are like that, all the time. I never expected things to end up as they are right now where they tried to adopt me. I didn't even understand what they were trying to do. I knew they were trying to take me to the United States, away from the baby's home [orphanage] and give me parents, which I never had. But I really didn't have a mature understanding about it. All I remember is they were very nice and friendly people.

I did not grow up an orphan in Uganda. I left the orphanage and went to live with Sylvia and Justinian Tamusuza, a family where I was fostered when I was nine years old and my biological parents were still living. I hear my father died in 2014. Last time I checked my mother was still living. When I went to visit them in 2012, my mother was not in good condition, living in poverty. That was my second time in my whole life to sit down and talk with my mother. She said she was going to die years before from an automobile accident but she didn't. I didn't have any connections with either my father or mother while growing up. I wasn't really an orphan, but in a way I guess I was if they abandoned me. The fostering system has some challenges, trying to figure out how you fit in. It helps if you have a blood connection and are part of their family. Being in boarding school helped me find friends. When I came back to Sylvia's home on break, it was good.

I went to different boarding schools. I wouldn't say they were Christian schools, but they did Christian things, like chapel and prayer. The schools were not church sponsored. It was just that someone started a school who was a Christian. I did my best, I am an average student, and school has always been challenging for me. I realize I had a problem with my left nostril and I could not breathe through it from birth. That made studying very difficult because I did not sleep through the night. I was able to get my nose opened in December, 2014 with an operation in Pittsburgh. My life is much better now because I can sleep.

When I graduate from Palm Beach Atlantic, in 2017, only God knows what my future will be. This is like my family for real. I would like being in my culture where I grew up, so it's really tearing me apart over which I should choose.

My relationship with the Lord is very important to me. I feel that, if I didn't have God, I wouldn't be where I am today. I live my life with hope and faith. A lot of people ask me how I made it. I just have a lot of hope and faith. Even if things go the way I don't want them to go, I just keep going. It's very important to me that I put Him first before everything. I had this concept from when I was little. If things are not right and I get sick or if things go bad or anything ever happens, God is always there in each and every way in my life. I try to live according to His expectations for me.

As far back as I can remember, I had this awareness of the Lord's presence in my life. When I was at the baby's home called Mustard Seed, I was really grateful I was there because they really taught us about God. I was young, but I really knew God. I try to explain it to people, that when you are young and people tell you about anything, you believe it. Like how people believe that Santa is real. They told me about God and I really believed in God so much. I pray and talk to Him all the time. I would pray if I had any problems at school or if I was crying, I would just talk to God.

Since we didn't have parents in that orphanage, and of course you had to compete for attention from all the workers there, it's really hard for them to reach out to all the kids there. Therefore, they introduced us to God and that was a great thing for them to do. I really took it to heart and I feel like maybe that is why I got here. I believed in God and continued being faithful to Him, even when I was a little kid. Even to get here I had to pray and tell Him what was happening when I was young.

Back in Uganda, I was going to a Catholic church because the family I was living with was Catholic. I didn't really have a church since I was in boarding school. I wouldn't have affiliated myself with church. I went to different churches and have been exploring.

My biggest surprise about the United States is the culture. Africa is more community-oriented. People are willing to meet other people. It is so hard here to do that. Everyone is disjointed and scattered. I like the people here, if you get to know them, they are really kind and sweet. The convenience of how to get things, the security, the good health system, are all well developed things. I like the schools here; the professors are really nice. I like my family here. They make things much better. I don't know what I would do if they weren't here. There are four other African students at Palm Beach. I was surprised there weren't more at first, but now I understand it is a private university and expensive. There are a lot of Haitians there, and they have a similar culture to what is in Africa.

I have brothers and sisters in Africa. I don't know them that well, but I knew I had them. When I visited my parents, I met them. I miss the culture and family atmosphere of my native Uganda. When I graduate, I want to work with an organization that reaches out to children in bad conditions, who really need help so I can just be there to support. I started working with younger children years ago, but as time went on, it developed into other ages. In school, I have enjoyed the humanities courses. I enjoy writing, though it takes a lot of time and effort. I enjoy research work, and also politics and civic engagement.

I stay in touch with people back in Uganda using Skype and text. I also saw Sylvia while she was here. I call her Mama and I call Janet Mom, too. I am blessed with multiple mothers.

Syvlia Nannyonga-Tamusuza

My name is Sylvia Nannyonga-Tamusuza. I met Janet in 2001 when I was graduating from the University of Pittsburgh. Coming to America was not easy, because my background isn't English, which we learn after becoming fluent in our mother tongue. I was at the University of Pittsburgh for four years and came out with a doctorate in ethnomusicology. In Uganda, I am the first female ethnomusicologist.

Ethnomusicology is the study of music to understand people and the study of people to understand music. That's the most concise definition I can give. I love music and love people, so my chosen field of study is how I can bring those two together. Obviously, people create music from a variety of influences – physical, psychological, cultural, and the like. I'm interested in knowing how these two interact – people and music – and how I can come to understand them more. Of course, when I am trying to understand people, I am also trying to understand myself. I am also aware that music has been used for good as well as for bad, but it's important to study the bad with the good. Knowledge is power, and if you have knowledge, then you have the ability to address the problem or issue.

Back home, I am teaching and do a lot of research. Right now, I have 18 publications and I have three that are in press. My dissertation was recognized as an outstanding dissertation in ethnomusicology, and it was published as a book by Routledge. I wrote and published on Catholic Church music, and published material on politics in music. I also did a research in Sweden and wrote about conceptualization of African music.

It has been my privilege to observe Janet and the progress of her teaching on the Orphaned Heart almost since the beginning. Janet has already referenced the concert in 2006 at Uganda Christian University. I have many recollections of that particular day. At one point the students in the audience didn't appreciate some of the aspects of the music, because we were singing in a classical style. They were more interested in a popular style. When they reacted, we were a little nervous about what was going on. At the end, someone made a comment and people were shouting. That led both Janet and me to wonder if anything of our message had gotten through to them.

At the conclusion of the show, we invited people to stay and give their comments. At that point, I was amazed because the message really came across, and many of them wanted to be a part of the Hope Fellowship, which we wanted to form to continue the discussion about rejection and the Orphaned Heart. There were so many wounded, even those who had the chance to go to the university, which of course indicated that they needed more than just an education if they were orphans.

During the after-the-performance discussion, I shared my experience with the love and care for my family's children, especially my own child of whom I was the legal foster parent. Despite the love I had given him, he was always so empty. One time he asked me what love is and how is it expressed. At that point, I had the idea for the Hope Fellowship. When Janet realized how large the problem was, she was fully onboard with whatever needed to be done to promote healing the Orphaned Heart.

My son was 11 months old when I adopted Him, although we do not call it adoption. In fact, adoption as it is known in the U.S. is not common at all in Uganda or throughout Africa, for that matter. In my culture, the terms fostering and foster parents are more common. Today, my son is 22.

When I first heard Janet's message, I thought it was wonderful. I told her that even if we give children education and all of the other things of life, without the spiritual connection, it is a wasted effort. I could not participate in helping to spread her message because I had many other things going on. Even today, I am so fully involved that I'm unable to be active for her, but I think it is so needed.

I must also be honest that my own spiritual life has changed since 2006. When I first worked with Janet, I was Catholic, but I left the church in 2011 and now I am born again. Therefore, I am looking at spiritual things from a very different angle today. So my approach to the Orphaned Heart dilemma is very different today than in 2006. Today, we are promoting having more Hope Fellowship chapters. In 2006, I was using a more Catholic approach, which did not include a strategy that employed Hope Fellowships.

Eventually, I realized there were gaps in my approach that relied more on private prayer and the sacraments, which is a Christian approach, although somewhat limited. Now I see more clearly what Janet is doing because of my deeper spiritual connection. It has also influenced me in the way I think of ministry, but also in how I teach at the University. After being born again, I look at the whole of life. As a professor, I have been confronted with many students who are having learning challenges because they are from broken families and are orphaned. I also have a ministry called Love and Care Family, and my approach in ministry has been deeply impacted by my relationship with Janet.

In fact, the term *being orphaned* is much broader than not having parents, and I have learned that students can suffer deep wounds from rejection even if they lived with their parents. I'm beginning to see how I can use more of Janet's material to deal with my students in the University. For example, God has blessed us to help two young men who were alcoholics and dropped out of school. God has given them a new life, and we are working to help restore their ability to function in life.

My ministry, the Love and Care Family, is about giving love and care to children who are not wanted or loved, even by other social organizations. We define a child very differently than the way children are elsewhere defined. For example, there is one young man who came to us when he was 18 years old, and wanted to go to school. Many projects would not allow him to do so. They would take him up to the age of 18, using the American or Western concept of a child. After that, he was considered an adult.

We gave that young man an opportunity to go back to school, and recently he graduated from college. I was giving a second chance to someone who probably wouldn't have gotten one anywhere else, but we also look to help vulnerable children who are much younger. Our focus is not on numbers, but is mostly on creating a person who is holistically healed — body, soul and spirit. We have small numbers, but we take them and provide another family for them to serve as a backup.

Let me give you another example. In our culture, marriage is important, and when you marry, you aren't just marrying a person, you are marrying their clan and all they represent. If someone is an orphan, then their partner is also orphaned in a sense because they are not marrying into a family. That is why we provide a surrogate family into which the partner can marry. Today, we have had two young men who have married under this arrangement.

In 2006, we sponsored a workshop for orphaned children. During the conference, one young man said it was difficult to think of marriage. (In our culture, the groom's family goes to the bride's family to "arrange" the marriage ceremony and other details.) This young man didn't have people to go with him. I have had to do this twice because young men had no family, except me, the grandmother, to stand for them.

When I teach, I see many many people who are impacted by rejection, but of course I can't go and overwhelm them with what I think they need. I create an opportunity where they are free to come and talk to me. At the same time, I am a very strict teacher who wants them to do the right things academically. Despite my classroom demeanor, I find that people come to me and share deep, personal things. Most of their parents were either divorced or separated or the students were born through extramarital relations. I find that many of them have been influenced by what they see in media or by their peers to think that if they take some pills or a drug, they will be calm and fine.

In fact, one student told me he takes the drug so he can be sane when he comes to my class. I try to explain to them that they're always absent, even when they are physically present in class. Most of those who come to me are truly seeking some kind of help. They desperately want and need to have someone to talk to them, and someone to help them out. My institution is a public one and, if I were in America, I wouldn't be able to do what I am doing. Many times, students would ask me how it is possible to do this or that, or do what I am doing? And I frankly tell them that it's only God who has enabled me. If they are interested, I can share with them about God. I make myself vulnerable and accessible – vulnerable in a sense that I share with them who and what I am, even if it may not be politically correct being in a public institution.

Simon Peter Dembe

My name is Simon Peter Dembe and I am a Ugandan, having grown up in Kampala. Unfortunately, my parents died when I was two years old, which is how I ended up in a baby's home [called an orphanage in the West]. My time in that home was hectic and hard. Probably what made it hard was the struggle to get food. Eventually, I was picked up by a doctor who was my auntie, Doctor Sylvia, and was taken to the Love and Care Home. I grew up there and from there was able to have an education up to a law degree that enabled me to get into the legal fraternity. I have a Master's of Divinity degree and I am teaching at the University while I also pastor a church.

I was first exposed to the Orphaned Heart teaching back in 2011. Dr. Sylvia asked me to take Janet Helms around Kampala. While we were in a taxi together, Janet was asking me about my life. I told her that my life had not been easy, but I gave glory to God that I had given my life to Christ. From that point on, I knew Jesus would take care of me. Janet listened and then said the Lord had laid something on her heart to help people like me. It was then that she introduced me to the healing of the Orphaned Heart.

She talked to me about many things, but the one that was most striking to me was that God is the Father to the fatherless. Then she talked about the hearts of men and how people were suffering with the spirit of an orphan. She explained how that spirit was impacting people's lives through the trauma and toxic shame. As Janet talked, I felt she was talking about me, because I was going through just what she described.

169

I had this shame about what happened in my life, because I had been sexually abused by my very own sister. I hated women because of how those sisters had treated me. I realized that if I understood the purpose and heart of Orphaned Heart Ministries, then it would be helpful first for me. When Janet took me through some inner healing prayers, I realized I was getting a release of the Holy Spirit and I was being healed.

After that encounter, Janet asked me to be the president of the Hope Fellowship at the Ugandan Christian University. I felt I was the right person because I knew what she was talking about and I knew what she was saying to people about how to overcome the broken heart. We had the first conference in July 2011 when she came with a number of people from the United States with a lot of material. That was the first conference I had ever attended in my life. They talked about many things, but they were literally talking about me. Long after that conference, I grew in the Lord and understood the reality that I am no longer an orphan. I used to look at myself as being both physically and spiritually orphaned. I needed the Orphaned-Heart message, and it has done a tremendous work in my life by God's grace.

The Hope Fellowship at the University brings together students who have lived through those orphaned situations, students who have been broken both spiritually and physically. Now when these students come together, we learn from the materials that we get from the conferences. Of course, out of their experience, many people have written about this concept. We have gathered a lot of material and put it into practice. After we have learned about these concepts in the fellowship, we conduct other clinics and conferences around the area.

So far, we have sponsored eight conferences, and I can't remember how many clinics we have held. We see it as our duty to reach out to the community by going door-to-door, and praying and encouraging people as we share this message that God wants to heal the Orphaned Heart. From those outreaches, we have actually seen people join the Fellowship and hope to start other Fellowships in different parts of the country, mainly in East Africa. We just had one Fellowship open in Rwanda.

Hope Fellowship meets every Friday from 7 to 9 PM, and also Sunday from 6 to 8 PM. As president, I organize the ministry, because we go to high schools, primary schools, and universities. It is incumbent on me to look out for meeting opportunities where we can present. I ask the teachers of those classes to allow us time to speak, then I also go to different churches, meeting the pastors and their wives and then meeting with the youth in churches and in schools.

We also go to prisons and hospitals. In hospitals, we mostly go in and pray with people, talk to them, and then support them as we can. If we have something, we may give them a kilo of sugar or a bar of soap and show them the love Christ has for them. And if any of them have not given their lives to Christ, one of our greatest mandates is to preach that there is healing in the name of Jesus Christ. When we accept Him as our Lord and Savior, we understand the power behind His stripes that were for our healing. So as president, my main task is to reach out with the message, while keeping the vision and mission of the ministry before the members and the public.

Recently we did some teaching on polygamy. We

have realized that in East Africa, many people are struggling because they come from polygamous families. We wrote a document about it and when we distributed it, we saw many people receive healing because there are many in those families, but God meets them where they are to minister to their hearts.

If I had to list the noticeable effects of the Orphaned Heart message in my life, I would start with true love. I was a person who would pretend to love people. I have seen that tendency in many of the Fellowship members. Today, I genuinely love others and take my ability to do so seriously because it will open many doors for ministry in the hearts of other people.

I used to feel rejected all the time. After all, I grew up knowing I was rejected and not loved. But after hearing Janet's message, I realized I am not actually rejected any longer. God loves me and I have to spread that love to the people. I no longer walk in rejection, but rather in acceptance. I know I am adopted in the family of God. I am an adopted son of our Lord Jesus Christ and of our Father in heaven.

The other thing that tormented me was the shame of my life. I thought everyone would know about my sexual abuse and battery, and how those ladies used to beat me with a cane like they would a cow. I carried a heavy load of toxic shame. I was concerned what people would think if they found out I was not a virgin. My words would be simple and few, and I would do many things to make sure people were unaware of my past. Today I talk about it freely, however, because I know when I talk about it, other people will get healed through my example and story.

My past had also traumatized me and, therefore, I

never participated much in school. I was always thinking about having to go home to be beaten. In fact, at the time I heard the Orphaned Heart message, I was at the bottom of my 100-student class! After my healing, my performance changed where my academics were concerned.

My trauma also affected how I related to other people. I would tend to stay by myself much of the time. If someone would love me, then I would love them back. If they did not treat me well, I could not handle it. Now if someone hates me or treats me badly, I know I can love them because that is a weapon Christ has given me — to love people without any strings attached.

We have a lot of exciting plans on the table for Orphaned Heart Ministries. First, we are planning to have the whole Fellowship expand beyond East Africa. Many countries outside East Africa have called us to bring our conferences there to start the ministry in their land. That will require a lot of money and we have not gotten it yet. Then we hope to start with a new Hope Fellowship in the various universities. We also hope to start a counseling project, because we know after hearing this message, some of the people have psychological challenges and need some help to find freedom. We want to have a counseling chamber to help people. Our mandate is to see that people come to the Lord Jesus Christ after we have gotten to know them and their challenges.

Orphaned Heart is a great ministry. From my perspective, I see what we are doing as God's ultimate plan to reach out to the Orphaned Hearted and broken hearted. Many people have a lot of acquaintances, but because they do not have a place to open up and share whatever they are going through, they end up getting into drug abuse and addictions. Some people get into homosexuality simply because their hearts have been broken. They want and need to find comfort, but they are choosing the wrong things. We have found a better way, and I want to devote my life to sharing the freedom I have found in the Orphaned Heart Ministries message and work.

This is Janet speaking, and now you understand why I am so committed to expand the impact that Orphaned Heart Ministries has in East Africa. These three testimonies are just a few of the many that I could include of people who have been touched by our message.

Epilogue

On February 16, 2016, I was close to completing this book when God woke me at 5 AM while I was in Florida. I went out on our porch where I had a front row view of lightning bolts that flashed across the sky, slicing through the night darkness, a canopy of holy light illuminating the earth below. For two hours I could not turn away from the awesome and riveting display of nature's power. That very night I had attended a Bible study that focused on the book of Romans, during which I was challenged to live under the new covenant of the Holy Spirit rather than the old covenant of the Law.

God was giving me a message during the study, and he was delivering the same message during the light show. We are no longer living under the curse of Adam. As children of God, we have all of the promises of God to claim, live, and enjoy. We no longer live under the dark cloud of fear and condemnation, as Paul reminded us: "There is no condemnation for those who are in Christ Jesus" (Romans 8:1). We must learn to live in the victory of what Christ accomplished on the Cross. Furthermore, I realized after watching that light show that I must teach people to stop living in the pain and sorrow of the Orphaned Heart once they are healed. They need to live in victory of the Cross and the presence of the Holy Spirit.

Suddenly, just like lightning across the sky, it became clear to me what the next step is to heal from the wound of the Orphaned Heart. We must embrace what it means to be a child of God, not just live in the place of a healed heart, but embracing all of what it means to be His child. When Jesus died on the cross, the Temple veil was torn in two and we now have access into the Holy of Holies (see 2 Corinthians 3:12-18). Living as a child of God embodies a vibrant relationship with God the Son, God the Father and the Holy Spirit.

When Jesus says in John 14:18, "I will no longer leave you as orphans; I will come to you," He meant that we were to live lives of total transformation. Jesus prayed for those whom God had given Him as He uttered His high priestly prayer in the seventeenth chapter of John. I entreat you to read that prayer in that chapter, and then to embrace what it means to live in victory as a child of God. That is my next passion: for God to transform the heart of the orphan to the heart of a child of God. What glory awaits us while living here on earth waiting for His Kingdom to come!

You, the reader, have just finished my story of how I came to identify the problem of the Orphaned Heart, and the remedy that God has shown me to address its effects. As you can see, I am open to any and all biblical techniques and insights that will add to what I know that can help others. Therefore, I have included my contact information at the end of this book so that you can get in touch with me with your own testimonies or insights into the issue of the Orphaned Heart and healing prayer. I would also welcome inquiries into how to sponsor a healing prayer workshop in your area, and look forward to partnering with you wherever you may live.

Finally, I have also included the website for the Kenya Christian Educational Partnership if you would like to contribute toward the cause of education in East Africa. You can check the site to learn of our new initiatives, as we use education as a tool to help heal Orphaned Hearts. Thank you for reading my story, and may the Lord set you free to help others be free as well.

Appendix One

Below is a section of my paper I compiled for my graduate degree from Trinity Seminary in Ambridge, PA. The thesis' topic was "Healing the Orphaned Heart in East Africa." This excerpt covers the reasons why the Orphaned Heart message has had such receptivity in East Africa.

VIII. East Africa is the ideal nexus of the circumstances most desirable for an inner healing of the soul to resolve the isolation and sadness of the orphan heart and spirit.

Christianity is rapidly growing and it is estimated that soon there will be almost a half billion Christians in Africa, predominately found in the Southern Hemisphere.[1] Heal-

---

[1] Thomas C. Oden, *How Africa Shaped the Christian Mind: Rediscovering the African Seedbed of Western Christianity* (Downers Grove: InterVarsity Press, 2007), 10.

ing of the Orphaned Heart is a Christian message and in the same way the Gospel is on fire in Africa, this message of healing can be spread.

In addition, there are five reasons why East Africa, spiritually, historically, culturally and sociologically is ready to receive this healing:

(1) *Christianity is in the DNA of East Africans and the Christianity of today is truly African, not Western in nature.* To bring the message of healing the Orphaned Heart, we need to consider the religious environment of East Africa. I contend that the foundation of the African Traditional Religion, which affects its culture in concert with the personal transformative power of the Gospel, is conducive to the receiving and the spreading of the healing of the Orphaned Heart and creating a new spiritual family of belonging. Christianity arrived on the continent centuries before the missionary movement of Europe in the 1800's. Thomas Oden asserts "Christianity would not have its present vitality in the Two-Thirds World without the intellectual understanding that developed in Africa between 50 and 500 C.E."[2] Christianity is in the DNA of the people. Arguably this could be a reason Christianity has been embraced. Let us not think it is simply a copy of what Western missionaries brought. Today African Christianity has its own identity, arisen out of distinctly African experience on African soil".[3]

(2) *Africans are foremost a spiritual people and believe in the power of the Holy Spirit in a tangible way.* African theologian Bediako believes the African response to Christ shows the significant impact the Gospel has had

---

[2] Oden, *How Africa Shaped*, 9.
[3] Oden, *How Africa Shaped*, 13.

on African life. "Far from obliterating the African primal view of things in its essentially unified and spiritual nature and replacing it with a two-tier modern Western view comprising sacred and secular dimensions, the Christian faith has in fact reinforced the African view. . . . New knowledge in science and technology has been embraced, but it has not displaced the basic view that the whole universe in which human existence takes place is fundamentally spiritual...God is an inner necessity for humankind."[4] They have affirmed their spirituality but this time focused on Christ. The Christology which emerges can be seen in titles such as 'Elder Brother' (H. Sawyer) and 'Ancestor, Great Ancestor'... grasps the reality of Christ in which all life is essentially conceived as spiritual." (176).

(3) The idea of family and community is for the development and healing of the whole, not of the individual. John Mbiti, an African theologian, describes the role of the individual:

> In traditional life, the individual does not and cannot exist alone except corporately. He owes his existence to other people, including those of past generations and his contemporaries. He is simply part of the whole.... Just as God made the first man, as God's man, so now man himself makes the individual who becomes the corporate or social man. It is a deeply religious transaction.... When he suffers, he does not suffer alone but with the corporate group; when he rejoices, he rejoices not alone but with his kinsmen, his neighbors, his relatives

---

[4] Bediako, Christianity in Africa. 122.

whether dead or living....The individual can only say: 'I am, because we are; and since we are, therefore I am'.[5]

Africans believe more in the spiritual world than in the physical reality. They understand the Orphaned Heart diagnosis and do not question that healing of this can happen through the power of the Holy Spirit. They also understand the family of God as a community which supports and defines the individual, and know Christianity offers the only solution to the healing, through Jesus' death and resurrection, so that we can be adopted into that family.

(4) The orphan crisis in East Africa brings attention and the search for a solution, both in Africa and also from the rest of the World. Africans *know* the spirit of the orphan resides in their countries because of the physical orphan crisis. They do not need to be convinced of the psychological and spiritual wounds from which they suffer. They have been looking for a way to heal the Orphaned Heart, but did not know terms, the theology, or the diagnosis of the orphan spirit. From my experience, when I have presented it to the people and the Church, it is received with open arms and fully embraced without question or hesitation. They themselves are the ones to share and spread it among their people. My belief is once it is received and implemented, it will spread to the rest of the world from the great healing which will be witnessed.

(5) The Structure of the Church in combination

---

[5] John S. Mbiti, *African Religions and Philosophy* (Oxford: Heinemann, 1969), 106.

with the strong grass roots efforts helps build and sustain the message. The Gospel has spread so quickly in Africa because of the power of the community. The message of Healing the Orphaned Heart is already beginning to spread as a grass roots effort (Refer to Section IX). The Ecclesiology of the Anglican and Catholic Church with its bishops and dioceses is well structured and respected. The combination will bring the people to the healing, but also, if the Church embraces this healing, the validity of the message will remain true and gain even more momentum.

－

Appendix Two

Theological Thread of
the Orphaned Heart in Scripture

I. Theological Insights from the Old Testament

A. The Fall

1) An immediate separation between God and man. Intimacy is gone.

2) The goal of Satan was realized: to change the mindset of man from Sonship to orphan mentality.[1]

3) Trust in God: replaced by fear. Man is separated from Father and Creator.

- Adam and Eve hid from the Lord.
- Knew they were naked. Shame entered for the first time and tried to cover themselves.

---

[1] Martin, *Displaying*, 199.

- God immediately knew they sinned (Gen 3:8-11). Their sin was exposed.

4) Humans are either sons of Satan or sons of God. (Eph 2:1,2). The LORD condemned the serpent, "I will put enmity between you and the woman and between your offspring and her offspring;..." (Gen 3: 15).

B. Sons of Abraham: Spirit of the Orphan/ Ishmael. Spirit of Sonship/ Isaac

Isaac: Covenantal blessing of sonship: (1) Abraham, and (2) marriage

"Sarah your wife shall bear you a son, and you shall call his name Isaac. I will establish my covenant with him as an everlasting covenant for his offspring after him." (Gen 17:19).

Ishmael: Blessing fruitfulness and multiplying – but no covenant (Gen: 16:10) (21:12-13)

God says, "As for Ishmael, I have heard you; behold I have blessed him and will make him fruitful and multiply him greatly....But I will establish my covenant with Isaac..." (17:20-21)

- Relationship with Abraham as their father as boys. Abraham was 86 (Ishmael 19:16). Abraham was 100 (Isaac 21:5). Abraham sent him and Hagar into the wilderness (21:14).
- At Abrahams' death – Isaac was blessed by God, Ishmael was not (Gen 25:9 and 25:11).

Hagar, was physically removed by Abraham from the home and put out to fend for himself in the desert. Ishmael would certainly have died if the Lord had not heard Hagar's plea, intervened and saved Ishmael. All of the feelings of being rejected by the human father would spring up in Ishmael: abandonment, sorrow, fear, lack of trust – all of the feelings associated with the Orphaned Heart. In Gen 25 at Abraham's death both Isaac and Ishmael were there to bury him (Gen 25:9). Isaac was blessed by God and Ishmael was not (25:11). Even at the death of their father, Ishmael was making an attempt to find his place as a son, yet he still did not receive the blessing.

An Observation on Islam: The heart of Islam is the heart of the orphan. In the discussion above on the Orphaned Heart of Ishmael and the circumstances of his birth and life, he was rejected by Abraham and even put out into the desert with his mother. Prophecies from Genesis 16:12 and 25:18 say, "And he (Ishmael) will be a wild donkey of a man, his hand will be against everyone, and everyone's hand will be against him. He settled in defiance of all his relatives"[2]. In Appendix A, the traits of the orphan heart are the same traits displayed by Islam, because they emanate from the view of God as a Master, not a loving Father. The founder of Islam, Mohammad, was also a full orphan who lost both his mother and father and was raised by an uncle. The purpose of this paper is not to fully prove this concept, but to point out the similarities for further reflection and prayer. If true, the more the world suffers from the Orphaned Heart, both in Africa and the West, the more people will turn to Islam because they are unable to understand the loving Father of Christianity.

II. The Meaning of Sonship and Spiritual Adoption Found in the New Testament.

All that began with the Fall of Adam and Eve in

---

[2] Brodowksi, *My Father*, 102.

the Garden is redeemed through the mission of Jesus with His proclamation "I will not leave you as orphans; I will come to you." (John 14:18) Jesus is speaking of his death and resurrection by which we can come into our full sonship. We are now able to have an intimate relationship with the God the Father again. It is through Jesus' sacrifice and his Ascension to the right hand of the Father, that the Holy Spirit has been sent to come and live in all believers.

The Father "offers costly love to each, out of his determination to have sons responding to love rather than merely servants obeying commands."[3]

The new spiritual family is the church, the body of Christ. Jesus said "whoever does the will of my Father in heaven is my brother and sister and mother." (Matt 12:50). The family unit has changed from the Old Testament model of covenantal relationship passed down through the biological family line. Jesus has restructured the spiritual family, now comprised of the sons and daughters of God who submit their will to the will of the Father. The church is now the family of God (John 10:16; Ephesians 2:18; 3:15; 4:6; 1 Peter 5:2-4).[4]

The Crucifixion: Jesus becomes the total orphan – he took on the sin of the world on the Cross and was separated from God the Father: "My God, why have you forsaken me?" (Mt 27:46; Mk 15:34). "God made him who had no sin to be sin for us, so that in him we might become the righteousness of God" (2 Corinthians 5:21).

The Resurrection: Jesus conquers sin, death and the devil, and as heirs of the Father we will celebrate at the

---

[3] Ken Bailey, *The Prodigal*, 88.
[4] Sproul and Mathison, *Reformation Study Bible*, 30.

great banquet table with our spiritual family.

III. The meaning of Sonship - Jesus' life as a human and as the Son of God.

As we view Jesus' life, the mystery of the Trinity is intertwined in the concept of Sonship. The mystery of the Trinity: "...Father, God in glory in heaven, the Son, God incarnate as man, the Spirit, God indwelling and empowering the Church and the believer, are not three gods side by side in uneasy competition with one another". We are reminded in Deuteronomy "Hear, O Israel: the Lord our God is one Lord" (Deuteronomy 6:4).[5] But there are still the three 'persons' of the Trinity, dependent upon each other for their identity. For example: each of "the terms, 'Father' and 'Son' presupposes the other and the relationship between them. The Father would not be Father unless he had a Son, and the Son would not be a Son unless had had a Father."[6] So in lies the mystery: they are one but separate.

All Old Testament writing about the Messiah: the prophesy, the law, and the Psalms were fulfilled in Jesus. (Luke 24:44; Romans 1:2-6). Jesus was born of virgin and adopted by Joseph into a human family. He had to be part of a human family as a son to enter into his inheritance as a Son of the Father. At the age of 12 he was found teaching but stayed with his human family until he was 30. Culturally a son was in apprenticeship at 12 until 30 when

---

[5] Smail, *The Forgotten Father*, 22.
[6] Thomas G. Weinandy O.F.M., *The Father's Spirit of Sonship: Reconceiving the Trinity* (Eugene, Ore.: Wipf & Stock, 2010), 66.
[7] Smail, *Forgotten Father*, 70.

they received the father's inheritance and began their own business.[8] Jesus became aware more fully of his separateness and understanding that God was his Father (Luke 2 story in the temple). His relationship with the Father was intimate and loving and through the Spirit had constant communication with Him, yet he submitted and was totally obedient to the will of the Father.

Jesus' Baptism is the beginning of the new relationship with the Father, as his voice is heard, calling him "My Son" and the Holy Spirit in the form of a dove descends upon him. Baptism represents death and resurrection. We must die to the spirit of the orphan. "Spiritual inheritance is obtained only after death."[9] It is here the Father names him as the "Son of God". He enters into the kleronomia, the inheritance of the Son, which is in the end death and resurrection.[10]

At the Lord's Supper Jesus says, "This is my blood of the covenant, which is poured out for many." (Mk 14:24). Notice the covenantal relationship – indicating the new membership into the family of God as sons and daughters of God is now through the blood of Jesus. Jesus prays for those that the Father gave to him in his Prayer: John 17 – The special place of those who the Father gave to Jesus.

Jesus calls the Father "Abba" for the first time when he prays in the Garden of Gethsemane, "Abba, Father, all things are possible for you. Remove this cup from me. Yet not what I will but what you will". (Mk 14:36). This reflects the OT relationship of following God's will – yet it

---

[8] Smail, Forgotten Father, 70.
[9] Brodowski, *My Father*, 119.
[10] Smail, *Forgotten Father*, 71.

is based on a deep intimate love. "The Father whom Jesus addresses in the garden is the one that he has known all his life and found to be bountiful in his provision, reliable in his promises and utterly faithful in his love."[11]

Via the Crucifixion, Jesus became the total orphan – he took on the sin of the world on the Cross and was separated from God the Father: "My God, why have you forsaken me?" (Matthew 27:46; Mark 15:34). "God made him who had no sin to be sin for us, so that in him we might become the righteousness of God" (2 Corinthians 5:21). "Atonement is directed towards God... On our behalf he is offering the active obedience that fulfills the Father's will and the passive obedience that willingly bows to the Father's judgment against sinners, because only thus can sinful men be acceptable to God" ... He is suffering the abandonment that his Father's judgment decrees for sinners, he is offering the trust and obedience that alone correspond to his Father's love, and when all is over he has to commend his work into his Father's hand and await his verdict upon it in his resurrection".[12] P.T. Forsyth puts it, "It gave man a new relation to God and God a new relation, though not a new feeling to man. It did not make God our Father, but it made it possible for the Father to treat sinners as sons."[13]

Through his Resurrection, Jesus conquers sin, death and the devil. His Sonship is different from our Sonship. It is he who in the uniqueness of his resurrection is designated the Son of God with power (Rom 1:4). He was the only Begotten Son. We were created and chosen as the

---

[11] Smail, *The Forgotten Father*, 36.
[12] Smail, *The Forgotten Father*, 122.
[13] Smail, *The Forgotten Father*, 123.

sons/daughters of God. When Jesus ascended into heaven he was seated at the right hand of the Father. Here he has the position of Ruler on God's behalf (Matthew 28:18, 1 Corinthians 15:27), accessible to all who call upon him (Hebrews 4:14) and to help them anywhere (Hebrews 4:16; 7:25; 13:6-8).[14]

The Eschatological meaning of Sonship is described by Ken Bailey from the Parable of the Prodigal Son when Jesus comes as both King and Judge. "The banquet the father offers to both his sons has eschatological meaning: The messianic banquet has begun. All who accept the father's costly love are welcomed as guests. Table fellowship with Jesus is the proleptic celebration of the messianic banquet of the end times."[15]

Conclusion from Scripture on the Orphaned Heart compared to the Orphan Spirit. Someone suffering from the Orphaned Heart "does not feel they have a safe place of value in the heart of a loving father."[16] The key to the Orphaned Heart is that it is an emotional wound resulting from the lack of love from a human father (and also the mother).

The 'orphan spirit' attaches to the wound of the Orphaned Heart and is present when "… someone does not feel safe in God the Father's love."[17] The symptoms of the orphan spirit are seen in a heart attitude (how the

---

[14] Sproul, R. C., and Keith A. Mathison. *The Reformation Study Bible: English Standard Version, Containing the Old and New Testaments.* Orlando, Fla: Ligonier Ministries, 2005. 1505.

[15] Ken Bailey, *The Prodigal and the Cross*, 88.

[16] Bruce Brodowski. *My Father My Son: Healing the Orphan Heart with the Father's Love.* (Matthews, NC: Carolinas Ecumenical Healing Ministries, 2010), 65.

[17] Brodowski, *My Father*, 106.

heart feels) and as a mental stronghold (what the mind thinks from the input of these feelings). To have such a condition, a person would exhibit traits including independence, hostility, contentiousness, and no sense of home, belonging or of being a son."[18]

Those suffering from the orphan spirit think of themselves only as servants, not as sons and daughters of the Father. They have to strive for all they have because they do not have the spiritual inheritance available only to sons and daughters of God the Father. To get what they can for themselves, they resort to competing, stealing, or begging. They also are afraid of intimacy because they have never been able to trust their father and therefore, have never learned to trust anyone, even God, Himself.[19]

In contrast to the spirit of the orphan, the opposite is possible. We can receive the 'spirit of Sonship' (or the Spirit of Adoption) by entering the family of God the Father through the saving work of Jesus Christ on the Cross. The Chart of "The Spirit of the Orphan Contrasted to the Spirit of Sonship" can be found in Appendix A.[20] This will aid in discernment and diagnosis to know the degree to which a person suffers from the spirit of the orphan or if the person has received the spirit of Sonship by accepting God the Father as their loving heavenly Father and received the spirit of Adoption.

Written by Janet Helms, January, 2016.

---

[18] Brodowski, *My Father*, 106.
[19] Brodowski, *My Father*, 119.
[20] Brodowski, *My Father*, 103 – 104.

Contact
The Author

Janet Helms

Donations by check can be made payable to the Anglican
Diocese of Pittsburgh (please place "Orphaned Heart
Ministries" in the memo line) or give through the
Orphaned Heart Ministries website below.

Orphaned Heart Ministries
P.O. Box 1223
Wexford, PA 15090
www.orphanedheart.org

jhelms@orphanedheart.org

Made in the USA
Middletown, DE
31 July 2017